# Citizenship Policies
# for an Age of Migration

## International Migration Publications from the Carnegie Endowment for International Peace

Caught in the Middle: Border Communities in an Era of Globalization
*Demetrios G. Papademetriou and Deborah Waller Meyers, Editors*

Citizenship Today: Global Perspectives and Practices
*T. Alexander Aleinikoff and Douglas Klusmeyer, Editors*

From Migrants to Citizens: Membership in a Changing World
*T. Alexander Aleinikoff and Douglas Klusmeyer, Editors*

*Monograph Series*

Reinventing Japan: Immigration's Role in Shaping Japan's Future
*Demetrios G. Papademetriou, Kimberly A. Hamilton*

Balancing Acts: Toward a Fair Bargain on Seasonal Agricultural Workers
*Demetrios G. Papademetriou, Monica L. Heppel*

Between Principles and Politics: The Direction of U.S. Citizenship Policy
*T. Alexander Aleinikoff*

Reorganizing the Immigration Function: Toward a New Framework for
  Accountability
*Demetrios G. Papademetriou, T. Alexander Aleinikoff, Deborah Waller Meyers*

Between Consent & Descent: Conceptions of Democratic Citizenship
*Douglas B. Klusmeyer*

Coming Together or Pulling Apart? The European Union's Struggle with
  Immigration and Asylum
*Demetrios G. Papademetriou*

Balancing Interests: Rethinking the U.S. Selection of Skilled Immigrants
*Demetrios G. Papademetriou, Stephen Yale-Loehr*

Converging Paths to Restriction: French, Italian, and British Responses to
  Immigration
*Demetrios G. Papademetriou, Kimberly A. Hamilton*

U.S. Refugee Policy: Dilemmas and Directions
*Kathleen Newland*

Managing Uncertainty: Regulating Immigration Flows in Advanced Industrial
  Countries
*Demetrios G. Papademetriou, Kimberly A. Hamilton*

# Citizenship Policies
# for an Age of Migration

T. Alexander Aleinikoff and Douglas Klusmeyer

*Codirectors of the Comparative Citizen Project*

Carnegie Endowment for International Peace
*Washington, D.C.*

Carnegie Endowment for International Peace
1779 Massachusetts Avenue, N.W., Washington, D.C. 20036
202-483-7600, Fax 202-483-1840
www.ceip.org

*To order, contact Carnegie's distributor:*
The Brookings Institution Press
Department 029, Washington, D.C. 20042-0029, USA
1-800-275-1447 or 1-202-797-6258
Fax 202-797-2960, Email bibooks@brook.edu

*Library of Congress Cataloging-in-Publication Data*

Aleinikoff, Thomas Alexander, 1952-
Citizenship policies for an age of migration / T. Alexander Aleinikoff and Douglas Klusmeyer.
  p. cm.
Includes bibliographical references and index.
ISBN 0-87003-187-2 (pbk. : alk. paper)
1. Citizenship. I. Klusmeyer, Douglas B., 1957- II. Title.
  JF801 .A427 2002
  323.6—dc21

                                                                    2002002965

*Typeset in Times Roman. Composition by AlphaWebTech, Mechanicsville, Maryland.*
*Printed on acid-free paper (85% recycled content) with soy inks by Malloy Lithographing,*
*Ann Arbor, Michigan*

09  08  07  06  05  04  03  02          5  4  3  2  1          1st Printing 2002

# Contents

# Foreword

MIGRATION HAS ALWAYS BEEN WITH US. Yet it size and political relevance have been rising steadily since the middle of the twentieth century and should continue to increase well into the twenty-first century. As migration swells, citizenship policy is crucial—to promote inclusiveness and integration, strengthen the rights and responsibilities of membership in the civic community, and reduce potential disputes between states over issues such as dual nationality.

Nearly four years ago, the Endowment's International Migration Policy Program launched a broad, comparative study of citizenship policy in liberal-democratic states. This project, which brought together leading researchers on citizenship and immigration from more than 20 countries, has already led to the publication of two well-received volumes of findings. The first, *From Migrants to Citizens* (2000), examines the citizenship laws and policies of 11 countries, as well as the evolving practices of the European Union. The second, *Citizenship Today* (2001), analyzes the legal and philosophical themes that inform citizenship policies

These two books form the foundation for this concluding volume, which offers practical policy recommendations on four of the principal aspects of citizenship: access to citizenship, dual nationality, political participation, and social welfare policy. Four working groups made up of scholars and experts from Europe and North America (under the guidance of T. Alexander Aleinikoff and Douglas Klusmeyer) spent a year preparing these recommendations, which are broadly applicable to liberal-democratic states around the world.

The Endowment's Migration Program grew significantly after 1989, when Doris Meissner, who later became commissioner of the Immigration and Naturalization Service, founded a small immigration project. In recent years, when it became clear that the program was bursting at the seams as one group within a larger institution, the Endowment helped relaunch it as the now independent Migration Policy Institute. Because this book is the culmination of work undertaken primarily under the Endowment's aegis and then completed by the Institute, it is being published as a joint project of our two institutions.

As with the previous two volumes, we express deep gratitude to the Ford Foundation for its generous support of the Comparative Citizenship Project, and to the Luso-American Development Foundation for helping the project hold useful authors' seminars and produce the three volumes.

JESSICA T. MATHEWS
*President*
Carnegie Endowment for International Peace

DEMETRIOS PAPADEMETRIOU
*Codirector*
Migration Policy Institute

# *Acknowledgments*

THE WORK FOR THIS VOLUME represents the culmination of a multi-year commitment to the comparative study of citizenship by the International Migration Policy Program of the Carnegie Endowment for International Peace. It was conducted with the generous support of the Ford Foundation and in full partnership with the Luso-American Development Foundation (FLAD) of Lisbon, Portugal.

Rainer Bauböck, Michael Fix, David Martin, and Patrick Weil served splendidly as chairs of their respective working groups and wrote the original drafts of each chapter appearing in this volume. Their outstanding work represents the backbone of this volume. In preparation for the volume, a workshop was held at the European University Institute in Florence, Italy, in April 2000. We wish to thank the European University Institute and Christian Joppke in particular for hosting this conference. We also extend our thanks to Susan Martin, Executive Director of Georgetown University's Institute for the Study of International Migration, for cosponsoring that event. The working group reports were discussed at a conference held in Lisbon in July 2000 that was hosted and financed by the Luso-American Development Foundation and held at their conference facilities.

In the preparation of this manuscript, Kerry Boyd helped with formating the chapters and filling out citations. We would also like to express our appreciation to Helena Arouca, Yasmin Santiago, Vitor Ventura, and Paula Vicente for coordinating the Lisbon working group meetings. Yasmin Santiago also deserves special mention for helping to coordinate the Comparative Citizenship Project from beginning to end with great skill and patience.

Final preparation of the manuscript owes much to Adria Armbrister, who also wrote the executive summary, copy editor Jacqueline Edlund-Braun, and Sherry Pettie of the Carnegie Endowment, who guided this volume through the publication process with her usual dexterity. Finally, we are grateful to the Ford Foundation for its generous support throughout this project. Without that Foundation's support and FLAD's commitment to sponsoring the three annual conferences and the subsequent publications, this project would not have been possible.

# Citizenship Policies
# for an Age of Migration

# Introduction

FOR MODERN LIBERAL-DEMOCRATIC STATES, citizenship has traditionally been the formal hallmark of full membership, and the overwhelming majority of residents automatically acquire this status at birth. As a collective bond of uniform legal status and a shared source of common rights and duties, citizenship offers a fundamental framework for both expanding the inclusiveness of our increasingly diverse societies and promoting cohesion amid this diversity. As the example of the European Union (EU) shows most clearly, however, the contours of this framework are becoming more differentiated, as membership within modern polities becomes more multilayered. Citizenship is not simply a form of belonging but also an important agency through which fundamental principles of fairness and justice in a polity are institutionalized and guaranteed. How a polity administers citizenship then is a powerful measure of its core commitments.

The arrival of large numbers of immigrants in developed states over the last several decades has led policy makers, advocates, and scholars to pay increasing attention to citizenship policies. High immigration levels are likely to persist long into the future. As the recent United Nations *Replacement Population* study suggests, most of the developed states will have to admit a continuing supply of immigrants if only to avoid a steady shrinkage in their native population's size (UN Secretariat 2000). Not only will most of these states decide to supplement their native workforces through immigration to support

1

their retirement systems, but many have now begun to compete for selectively trained immigrants to fill labor market niches.

In an era of large-scale migration, issues of membership become increasingly complex. Migration makes host societies culturally and socially more diverse and makes the legal status among members (old and new) more differentiated. States that have witnessed high levels of immigration in recent years are thus facing new and difficult questions regarding citizenship policies. When, and how, for example, should citizenship be extended to new immigrants? Should dual nationality be embraced, tolerated, or discouraged? Which rights and opportunities should be limited to citizens; which should also be made available to immigrants? These sorts of questions reflect that citizenship status provides a greater range of rights, duties, and legal protections than the status of alien, but how closely the two statuses should approximate one another remains unsettled.

Historically, state laws and practices have varied widely, yet citizenship regimes of liberal democracies have generally featured the following elements: birthright citizenship, routes to citizenship through naturalization, disfavor of dual nationality, and policies that limit certain rights and opportunities to citizens. In recent years, the old understandings have come under increasing pressure, and citizenship rules have undergone significant—if generally unnoticed—transformation. This is perhaps most noticeable in the growing convergence among states regarding policies of acquisition of citizenship. Such policies are usually classified in two broad categories: *jus soli*, which confers citizenship based on birth on state territory; and *jus sanguinis*, which confers citizenship based on descent. *Jus sanguinis* states typically grant citizenship to children born to citizens outside state borders, whereas *jus soli* states limit the transmission of citizenship outside their borders in various ways. In recent years many *jus sanguinis* states—faced with several generations of foreign nationals residing within their borders—have adopted policies that grant citizenship to children born to certain classes of immigrants; at the same time, some states have altered *jus soli* rules to limit birthright citizenship to children born to settled (not temporary or undocumented) immigrants. Increasingly, these kinds of changes have made it difficult to classify states as falling into one category or the other.

So too policies toward dual nationality in many states have changed dramatically. For most of the twentieth century, a majority of states sought to restrict dual citizenship, based on the view that multiple citizenships created personal and diplomatic complications. However, high levels of immigration and other factors have made instances of dual nationality far more common, and states have begun to search for policies that *manage*, rather than *prevent*, plural citizenships. Indeed, a number of states have adopted new rules that affirmatively authorize dual nationality—for instance, by permitting citizens to naturalize in another state without losing the citizenship of their state of origin.

Finally, states in which a significant percentage of the population is of foreign nationality are rethinking traditional policies that have allocated rights and benefits based on citizenship status. The general trend is toward affirming that settled foreign nationals should have social welfare rights largely comparable to those extended to citizens, and there is increasing recognition of local franchise rights for immigrants.

The causes of these changes are many. The impact of immigration has already been noted. But developments in human rights law, new norms regarding gender equality, free trade regimes, and the establishment of transnational communities have also played a significant role. In the face of these developments, some have argued for reasserting citizenship as a way to foster a unified national identity and a bond among state members in multicultural polities; from this perspective, citizenship provides a common core, a safe harbor, in a world where cross-national and international pressures challenge traditional conceptions of the nation-state.

For as long as there are national states, citizenship will remain an important status. Citizenship, at its best, embraces the ideal of shared, universal rights. Attaining the status of citizenship holds forth the promise of equality with all other citizens. Citizenship also denotes the members of an intergenerational project, who are committed to honoring a past and promoting a better future for generations to follow.

Yet citizenship policies also, inevitably, have an exclusionary side. Not all can be members, and with membership—in the scheme of human affairs—generally come benefits and opportunities not open to nonmembers. The preferential treatment of citizens may seem natural, but it is arguably in significant tension with premises of liberal democracies that affirm a right for persons to participate in the government that exercises power over them. Settled immigrants pay taxes, support schools, attend places of worship, and—in a number of states—serve in the military. In short, they generally function in society in ways almost indistinguishable from citizens. On what grounds, then, it might be asked, can a liberal democracy refuse to extend them rights offered to citizens?

The competing considerations pose a daunting task to policy makers. Is it possible to both affirm the importance and centrality of citizenship in a liberal democracy and at the same time lower barriers to its acquisition, respect dual nationality, and extend rights to settled immigrants comparable to those granted to citizens? The tension here, it should be noted, may be somewhat more apparent than real. Making citizenship available on reasonable terms is surely in the interests of both the receiving state and settled immigrants. And recognizing social, economic, and political rights for resident immigrants will likely ad-vance their effective integration and participation in the state of settlement—providing a bridge to and training for the robust citizenship that democracies seek to foster. It cannot be contested, however, that crafting reasonable and forward-looking citizenship polices in a world of growing complexity requires a delicate balancing of the fundamental commitments of liberal democracies.

In 1997, the International Migration Policy Program of the Carnegie Endowment for International Peace established the Comparative Citizenship Project to develop proposals for citizenship policy in advanced, industrial, lib-eral-democratic states. In developing proposals, we undertook a three-year re-search project to examine how liberal-democratic states around the globe have been addressing the challenges that immigration poses for citizenship policies. This comparative approach has enabled us to identify important trends toward convergence among these states in crucial areas such as the strengthening of alien rights and the liberalization of citizenship acquisition rules. A compara-tive approach has also provided an effective means to test particular assump-tions that underlie various state policies. The United States, for example, has always regarded an exclusive loyalty oath as an indispensable requirement for naturalization, but many other liberal-democratic states have found that this requirement is unnecessary as an expression of allegiance. Finally, a compara-tive approach offers a broad framework for identifying "best practices" that states may borrow from one another.

The Citizenship Project has been a strongly collaborative endeavor that has drawn extensively on the talents and expertise of a diverse array of interna-tional scholars and policy analysts. This endeavor has proceeded in three stages.

In stage one, leading scholars prepared substantial monographs on citizen-ship laws and policies in eleven states (Australia, the three Baltic States, Canada, Israel, Japan, Mexico, Russia, South Africa, United States) and the European Union. The collection of these monographs has been published under the title: *From Migrants to Citizens: Membership in a Changing World* (Aleinikoff and Klusmeyer 2000).

Stage two focused on comparative patterns and trends among a range of states and considered such issues as alien rights, strategies of integration, gender and citizenship, welfare policies, and "transnational" citizenship. A selection of pa-pers from this stage has been published in a volume entitled *Citizenship Today: Global Perspectives and Practices* (Aleinikoff and Klusmeyer 2001).

In stage three, four working groups of senior experts, scholars, and policy analysts developed specific policy recommendations on issues identified dur-ing our research. The working groups prepared concrete policy recommenda-tions in four areas: (1) access to citizenship through reformation of birthright and naturalization rules; (2) dual nationality; (3) political rights of settled foreign nationals and citizens; and (4) restrictions on noncitizens access to social benefits and economic opportunities. The working groups were chaired, respectively, by Patrick Weil, David A. Martin, Rainer Bauböck, and Michael Fix, who took the laboring oar in drafting this report.* There was consensus among working group members regarding the project's broad policy directions and proposals. Specific recommendations reflect widespread—although not always universal—agreement among project members.

One of the guiding normative goals of any modern liberal-democratic model of citizenship should be the promotion of participation by all (lawfully settled) individuals and groups within a polity on a fair and equitable basis. Expanding opportunities for active participation in the economic, political, and social life of a society enables individuals and groups with diverse interests, backgrounds, and perspectives to contribute most fully to the material and cultural enrichment of all. Through engaging in these opportunities, members strengthen their concrete linkages to one another and deepen their most basic stakes in the general welfare of their communities. In affirming this goal, we do not seek to minimize the many challenges that negotiating a balance between diversity and cohesion has always involved, but these challenges are an inevitable feature of modern pluralistic societies. In an era of high migration, these wide-ranging challenges will not diminish, but the most successful societies will be those who meet them squarely with confidence in the robustness of their liberal-democratic ideals.

\* \* \*

Because terminology varies among regions and states, we would like to be precise about the categories used to describe groups of migrants and citizens. In this study, the term *immigrant* refers to a person who has left his or her state of origin, is residing in another state, and has not naturalized in that state; that is, an immigrant is a foreign-born noncitizen in the receiving state. *Foreign-born* persons may be either noncitizens or naturalized citizens; they constitute the *first generation* in the receiving state. The terms *second generation* and *third generation* refer to the children and grandchildren, respectively, of immigrants, born in the receiving state; they may be citizens or noncitizens. *Communities of immigrant origin* (sometimes referred to as *ethnic minorities*) are communities constituted by immigrants and their descendants; they include both noncitizens and citizens.

---

*The membership of the working groups appears in appendix II.

# CHAPTER ONE

# Access to Citizenship

DEMOCRATIC POLITIES have traditionally regarded citizenship as fundamental in the distribution of important rights and benefits. Not surprisingly, then, access to citizenship has been subject to comprehensive regulation. Modern liberal-democratic states have used different kinds of mechanisms and criteria to control access to citizenship or nationality.[1] The standard approach to classifying access rules has been to contrast regimes based on *jus soli* (making birth on the sovereign's territory the crucial determinant) with those based on *jus sanguinis* (making descent from a parent with nationality the crucial determinant). In practice, however, this distinction matters less than is usually supposed because the vast majority of persons attain citizenship based on birth in the territory of a state of which their parents are citizens. Accordingly, the key questions about the acquisition of citizenship status arise with respect to newly admitted residents, their immediate family members, and their descendants. Even as to these categories of person, modern changes in both *jus soli* and *jus sanguinis* regimes have blurred the distinctions between the two: some *jus soli* states have modified their rules to bestow nationality only on children born to citizens or lawful permanent immigrants within state territory; and some *jus sanguinis* states now grant citizenship to third-generation children born in the state. As we will describe below, there is a marked movement toward a convergence of citizenship acquisition rules among liberal democracies.

We propose a new classificatory approach that recognizes and affirms the trend toward convergence—an approach that adopts *generations* as the category of analysis. Briefly put, we recommend that third-generation foreign nationals be entitled to citizenship at birth and that second-generation foreign nationals have access to virtually automatic citizenship (these recommendations, of course, would alter policies only in states that currently follow *jus sanguinis* principles). We also propose that first-generation children who immigrate to a state at an early age be considered as part of the second generation in the application of citizenship rules. (This recommendation suggests changes in policies for both *jus soli* and *jus sanguinis* states.) Finally, we propose that naturalization standards for first-generation immigrants strike a reasonable balance between legitimate state selection criteria and the interests of would-be citizens in obtaining naturalization. Furthermore, naturalization procedures should be precise and objectively administered.

Addressing these questions involves a broad range of issues that (among others) implicate the deepest meanings of citizenship, assumptions about socialization and identity, the claims of individual rights and political justice, the interests of family unity, and the collective claims of cultural groups. We believe that a "generations approach" can appropriately respond to, and reflect, these values. The approach further recognizes that the admission and settlement of newcomers is a dynamic process, and that in crafting citizenship rules states may legitimately take into account the stages in that process.

### Generational Approach

Our analysis is premised on a commitment that we should make explicit: it is desirable that immigrants and their descendants become citizens and have the right to become citizens. This commitment may be defended as a matter of the moral entitlements of the individuals themselves, as a necessary implication of the state's commitment to democratic norms, as a socially advantageous public policy, or as a combination of all three factors. The first is based on the importance to the individual of state membership in a world of nation states.[2] The second consideration flows from the idea that individuals have a right to participate in the political system that rules them and that citizenship is generally viewed as an appropriate marker of national political rights.[3] The third consideration—public policy grounds—identifies a range of individual and state interests. For example, naturalization and citizenship at birth are likely to aid in the process of integration. Further, to admit foreigners to state territory but not permit them or their children to become citizens might lead to the establishment of foreign enclaves whose population would depend on foreign states. In stating that there is a duty on states to make citizenship available to immigrants, we also recognize a concomitant obligation on immigrants to demonstrate progress toward integration when seeking citizenship, an issue we will address below in our discussion of naturalization norms.

We further assume in this chapter that the strength of the norm for including people as citizens is related to the length of time they and their immediate ancestors have been living in the society. This view is widely shared and corresponds in important ways to existing practices. In addressing the issue of access to citizenship, therefore, we propose to distinguish between the *first generation* (people born and raised in another country who immigrate to a new country as adults) and their descendants in the *second and third generation* (the immigrants' children and grandchildren born and raised in the country to which the first generation has immigrated). We modify this traditional categorization of immigrant generations in one important respect. Typically the foreign-born minor children of immigrants who immigrate at an early age are classified as members of the first generation (sometimes referred to in the sociological literature as the 1.5-generation). Because these children spend their formative years in the country of immigration, we propose to include them in our definition of the second generation; that is, in our view, they are not meaningfully distinguishable from children born to immigrants in the country of immigration.[4]

The general norm we propose is that nationality laws should provide automatic or near-automatic access to citizenship to the second and third generations. For these groups, the acquisition of citizenship should be rapid, secure, and nondiscretionary. The third generation should simply be attributed citizenship at birth. The second generation should acquire citizenship at birth or somewhere between birth and adulthood. For the first generation, we propose criteria for naturalization that reasonably balance state and individual interests and that minimize administrative discretion in the naturalization process.

## Policy Recommendations for Three Generations

### Third Generation

The third generation is composed of the grandchildren of the first generation. Members of the third generation are born in a country in which their parents have been born, raised, and continue to live. The vast majority of the third generation—like the children of citizens—will make their lives in their country of birth. Because their parents have already been socialized in the country of immigration, no justification exists for waiting until the third generation is raised and socialized before making them citizens. We therefore propose that the third generation acquire citizenship at birth.

This proposal is by no means a radical one. It corresponds to existing practice or trends in most liberal-democratic countries. *Jus soli* states, of course, generally embrace such a rule. But more than is usually recognized, it is frequently the rule in *jus sanguinis* states as well. First, many children in the third generation acquire citizenship at birth via *jus sanguinis* rules because one or both of their parents (in the second generation) acquired citizenship before the children are born. Furthermore, a number of *jus sanguinis* states have explicit rules conferring citizenship on third-generation children at birth. Such rules have been formally included in the nationality laws of Belgium since 1992, France since 1889, the Netherlands since 1953, and Spain since 1990.[5]

### Second Generation

For the second generation, their socialization has taken place or will take place in the country of immigration. They are, in all practical respects, members of the society in which they reside. Their legal status, we believe, ought to comport with the social facts: They are entitled to citizenship either at birth or at some point during their childhood. We recognize that the situation of children born to immigrants as well as the traditions and values of their countries of residence may vary state to state. Accordingly, so long as an entitlement to citizenship for the second generation is affirmed, a range of acceptable policies effectuating that entitlement is imaginable. We consider below several alternatives.

*Citizenship at Birth.*    One way of granting citizenship to most of the second generation is to have an automatic *jus soli* rule—citizenship to any person born on the territory—as one component of nationality law. The United States and Canada have policies of this kind. An automatic *jus soli* rule precludes an ongoing transmission of noncitizen status from generation to generation. Moreover, under such a rule, children know from an early age that they are full legal members of society, which can have a positive impact on their sense of belonging and thus on their integration. This approach also minimizes room for discretion or ambiguity. From an administrative perspective, the sort of proof required to establish that one was born on the territory is typically easy to acquire because the administrative procedures surrounding birth records are usually well established and well organized.

The disadvantage of an automatic *jus soli* rule is that it is underinclusive in some respects and overinclusive in others. It is underinclusive in not granting citizenship to those members of the second generation who arrive as very young children and spend their formative years in the country of immigration. Despite the usual view that automatic *jus soli* regimes are all-inclusive, in fact, they typically treat such children as members of the first generation, thereby requiring them to go through the naturalization process with their parents to attain citizenship.[6] As we describe below, we believe that such children merit an entitlement to citizenship that is rapid, nondefeasible, and nondiscretionary.

An automatic *jus soli* rule is also arguably overinclusive to the extent it bestows citizenship on children born to parents who are visitors or temporary residents in a state, who have no intent or desire to remain in the state or raise their children there. Such overinclusiveness raises three concerns.

First, it means that some people acquire citizenship even though their only tie to the society is the geographic accident of their place of birth. This concern is valid; but, importantly, it has little significance in terms of integration of immigrant generations. If the parents of these children become permanent residents and their children grow up in the society, they would in time have a moral claim to citizenship. In this circumstance, the automatic *jus soli* rule has simply accelerated an outcome that ought to have occurred anyway. If the parents return home, the children's newly acquired citizenship is normally of no real significance, except that it occasionally opens opportunities for the person later in life that would not otherwise be available. In either circumstance, the extension of citizenship at birth to some who have no strong claim to it at that moment does not create any serious social problem. In the United States and Canada, automatic *jus soli* rules have had and continue to have a powerful and favorable impact on the integration of generations of children of immigrants.

The second concern is that the institutionalization of an automatic *jus soli* rule in a developed state might create incentives for people from developing states to enter without authorization (or to overstay authorized visas) to have their children born in the developed country. Despite repeated invocation of this claim, there is scant evidence to support it. The vast majority of immigrants who enter states illegally do so to obtain work, join family, or flee persecution or civil strife. We seriously doubt that a desire to bear citizen children in the receiving state adds much to these incentives.

The third concern is that an automatic *jus soli* rule may influence other immigration norms regarding family reunification in undesirable ways. That is, states may adopt tougher rules on family unification if it is believed that undocumented immigrants are giving birth to citizen children to secure relief from removal. For example, in the United States and Canada, noncitizen parents of minor citizen children may be deported even though the children themselves are not deportable. In Europe, by contrast, where it is generally not possible for children of unauthorized immigrants or even legal temporary residents to acquire citizenship at birth, it is much more difficult to deport the noncitizen

parents of citizen children. Thus, under French law, parents who are legal guardians of minor citizens are protected against deportation. Because birth in the
territory does not bestow citizenship, there is less concern that undocumented
migrants may try to "manufacture" equity by having children.

It remains an open question whether these three concerns, separately or in
combination, are sufficiently compelling to warrant the modification of automatic *jus soli* laws in states that already have them. Some states such as Australia and the United Kingdom that formerly had automatic *jus soli* laws have
altered them to limit the automatic attribution of citizenship at birth to the children of citizens and permanent residents. These sorts of arrangements are defensible in principle, provided that they are coupled—as they have been in
these cases—with other provisions for the automatic attribution of citizenship
to those who are born and raised in the society.

In other states such as Canada and the United States, proposals have been
made to modify automatic *jus soli* rules through legislation or judicial interpretation. To date, none of these proposals has succeeded. In the United States,
where the *jus soli* rule has traditionally been interpreted to flow from the Fourteenth Amendment to the Constitution, a change would require either a constitutional amendment or a strong reinterpretation of the meaning of the clause.
Because of the symbolic significance of the Fourteenth Amendment, good reasons—perhaps even compelling reasons—exist for resisting any change. In
Canada, where the change could be instituted through ordinary legislation and
where the *jus soli* tradition does not carry the same historic associations, the
reasons for resisting change are less powerful; still, the *jus soli* rule is con-
nected historically with a welcoming stance toward immigrants.

*Citizenship Based on Birth Plus Residence.*    Another strategy for secur-
ing citizenship for the second generation is to adopt a *jus soli* rule that requires both birth in the territory and either residence of a child for a specified
period prior to adulthood (as in France) or lawful residence of a parent (as in
Australia, Germany, and the United Kingdom). This approach partially ad-
dresses concerns regarding the overinclusiveness of an automatic *jus soli* rule.
If citizenship is granted based on a child's residence in the state prior to majority, then that child will have spent his or her formative years in the state. If
citizenship is granted based on a parent's lawful permanent residence, then—
in many states—the parent will have spent a significant period of time in the
state.[7] In either case, children born to those legally present on a temporary
basis will leave when their parents do and are unlikely to have a claim to
citizenship. Similarly, children born to unauthorized immigrants do not automatically gain citizenship at birth. A number of states that did not previously

have *jus soli* rules have adopted this sort of qualified rule—rather than an automatic *jus soli* rule—in an effort to promote the inclusion of the second generation (examples include Germany and the Netherlands). And, as noted above, some states that previously had automatic *jus soli* rules have also gravitated in this direction.

Several possible variations of this approach exist in theory and practice. The number of years of residence required either for the parent or for the child may vary; so too may the range of the relevant years (such as years from birth or years between six and eighteen). Citizenship may be granted immediately upon the completion of the specified residency requirement or upon attaining a specified age (such as eighteen). Citizenship may be made contingent upon other behavior (no criminal record, completion of school). And it may be bestowed automatically upon completion of the conditions or only upon application (so that fulfillment of the conditions generates an entitlement rather than the status itself). If citizenship is granted automatically, the individual may or may not have a right to refuse the citizenship beyond whatever right of expatriation citizens by birth possess.

States have combined these elements in different ways. France, for instance, permits optional acquisition of citizenship under certain conditions at a younger age and automatic acquisition at a later age (with a right of refusal). By contrast, the recent reform of German nationality law includes a *jus soli* provision for the second generation on the condition of a legal and permanent residence of the parents of at least eight years, and it requires recipients of citizenship under this provision to renounce all other citizenships by the age of twenty-three or forfeit German citizenship.[8]

A "birth-plus" approach for the second generation, however, raises new problems. Even the least demanding residential requirement introduces an additional administrative requirement—not only proof of birth but also proof of residence, which is not always easy to establish with regard to preschool children. Even where school records are easy to obtain for children between the age of six and eighteen, the requirement nonetheless sends a message about the contingency of the children's acceptance into the political community until the conditions are satisfied. Additional requirements introduce other complications. For example, where acquisition of citizenship is automatic after a certain number of years, should the child be required to be currently residing in the state when citizenship is bestowed? (Such a case might arise if a child's parents resettle the family outside the country after years of residence there.)

Furthermore, the birth-plus approach may still be seen as overinclusive. For example, where citizenship follows from birth to a lawful permanent resident, a child may attain citizenship at birth but nonetheless spend his or her formative years outside the state if the parents choose to return to their country of origin for a period of time.

A crucial question for evaluating alternatives must be how well a proposed approach promotes integration of the second generation. We believe that a birth-plus approach with the following elements is likely to adequately pursue that goal: acquisition of citizenship should be automatic, rather than dependent upon the action of the individual;[9] it should be contingent only upon residence, rather than renunciation of other citizenships or noncriminal behavior (since such criminal conduct may reasonably be understood as the product of living in the country of birth); and residence requirements must be reasonable (such as ten years before eighteen or six years of schooling).

*Rules for a Broader Definition of the Second Generation: Residence Alone.* Neither an automatic *jus soli* rule nor a birth-plus rule provides citizenship to children who take up residence in a country at an early age with immigrant parents. As noted above, we believe that these children should be included in the second generation. Clearly, rules that require birth in the state make citizenship (other than by way of naturalization) impossible for this class of children. It is difficult, however, to distinguish their case from that of children born to immigrants in the country of settlement. They seem as likely to spend their formative years in the country in which they reside. Nor does their possession of citizenship in their parents' home state provide a substantial ground for distinction. The place where one is raised is normally far more important to one's interests, attachments, and life plans than the place where one is born (if they differ). Furthermore, we believe that a receiving society has a responsibility to provide and ensure civic integration of settled immigrants—particularly immigrant children, who are not likely to be integrated members of another society. It is thus no more reasonable to make citizenship contingent upon some independent measure of commitment or degree of integration for immigrant children, as it would be for other members of the second generation.

We recognize the strength of these considerations, yet we also understand that birth has traditionally played the major role in the assignment of citizenship—either birth on a state's territory or birth to citizen parents; that is, states are primarily communities of descent. It thus might be argued that to extend citizenship to a second generation defined to include foreign-born children of immigrants is simply a step too far.

We would urge those who come to this quick conclusion to give it more thought. Some states, it should be recognized, already take a further step in granting citizenship to any person born on their soil—no matter the status of the parents. Furthermore, there appears to be a global shift away from strict *jus sanguinis* citizenship rules. Germany provides a compelling example: Although it had a strong tradition of *jus sanguinis* and did not consider itself a country of immigration, it recently adopted a *jus soli* approach for children born to settled legal immigrants. This reform shows that states may be more ready to transcend tradition than might be supposed, if changed conditions so merit.

We believe that the strong likelihood of socialization in the state of residence combined with a goal of effective integration of immigrants supports a broadened definition of the second generation to include foreign-born young children who accompany their immigrant parents. To accommodate this class, states ought to recognize the citizenship of such children if they have received significant social or educational formation in the state. This recommendation, of course, applies only to foreign-born children, not to persons who enter as immigrants at an older age or have not spent their formative years in the state of residence. More precisely, we recommend that foreign-born children who, during their childhood, (1) have received six years of schooling in the state of residence or (2) have spent ten years of residence in the country be deemed to have satisfied these criteria.

As stated, this recommendation would apply to foreign-born children irrespective of their immigration status or the status of their parents. The reasons we have identified in support of the proposal—early socialization and the promotion of integration—would appear to have force whatever the status of the child. Nonetheless, other policy considerations also come into play. Although we doubt that many pregnant women illegally immigrate to *jus soli* states to give birth, we find it more plausible that a flat rule entitling all foreign-born children to citizenship after a period of years could serve as an incentive to illegal entry. Furthermore, states that have recently moved from *jus sanguinis* to *jus soli* regimes have required that children be born to permanent resident immigrants in lawful status of several years' duration to receive citizenship at birth.

Accordingly, our recommendation expanding the second generation to include foreign-born children applies primarily to children in a lawful status or who have parents in a lawful status in the state. States with automatic *jus soli* rules may well opt to go farther—that is, to grant citizenship to long-staying foreign-born children irrespective of status (just as children born in such states are citizens at birth irrespective of the status of their parents). Other states may want to fold the expanded definition into their general approach for acquisition of citizenship. Thus, if a state requires lawful permanent resident status for the parent before recognizing *jus soli* citizenship of children born in the state, so too it might reasonably decide that foreign-born children who accompany lawful immigrant parents should be recognized as citizens after a period of years.

*First Generation: Naturalization Policies*

When we turn to the first generation of immigrants—people who have moved as adults to the new country—the consensus on incorporating them into the citizenry seems much less secure. Differences over what is appropriate or permissible to require as conditions of naturalization are common. Nevertheless, less disagreement among states exists than one might imagine on the basic issue of making citizenship available to people who have settled permanently.

An examination of state practice offers the clearest way to demonstrate the narrowness of these disagreements. Our overview focuses on general requirements for naturalization as well as waivers and modifications of those requirements for particular categories of immigrants.

Each of the states in our study requires some period of residence before naturalization.[10] (See table 1 for specific requirements in selected countries.) The maximum period of residence required is ten years (Austria, Greece, Italy, Luxembourg, Netherlands, or Spain); the minimum is three (Belgium, Canada). No other criterion is universal. Almost all states require some evidence of acquisition of an official or dominant language. A few states also require evidence of knowledge of the culture or history or institutions of the country, often by means of a written test. Many states mandate the absence of a (serious) criminal record, and some demand separate or additional evidence about the applicant's character. Most states impose fees for naturalization—some quite substantial fees. Some states require proof that the applicant is able to maintain himself or herself economically. Finally, some states require new citizens to take an oath of allegiance or some other formal commitment that may include renunciation of other citizenship held by the applicant (see chapter two for a detailed discussion of renunciation requirements).

*Application Criteria.*    We have recommended that citizenship for the third and second generations be considered an entitlement. But the considerations supporting those proposals apply with far less force to first-generation immigrants, who have undergone social formation outside their new country of residence. We believe that it is reasonable to require these immigrants to apply for citizenship.

Criteria for naturalization should be clear, limited, precise, and objective. Importantly, criteria should not be open to arbitrary administrative discretion; states should construct the criteria so that there are objective indicators of when they have been met. Meeting the criteria should generate a legal entitlement to naturalization. In addition, administrative decision should be subject to judicial review.

Table 1. *Naturalization Requirements in Selected Countries*

| Country | Residence | Knowledge of History | Knowledge of Language | Loyalty Oath | Sufficient Income | Good Character | Absence of Conviction | Renunciation of Prior Citizenship |
|---|---|---|---|---|---|---|---|---|
| France | 5 years | — | Yes | — | Yes | Yes | Yes | — |
| Germany | 8 years | — | Yes | — | Yes | — | Yes | Yes |
| Netherlands | 10 years; must reside for 5 consecutive years before application | — | Yes | — | — | — | Yes | Yes |
| Spain | 10 years | — | — | — | — | — | — | — |
| United Kingdom | Permanent residence or Crown service for 5 years | — | Yes | — | — | Yes | Yes. | — |
| United States | 5 years | Yes | Yes | Yes | — | Yes | Yes. Criminal convictions leading to more than a one-year sentence are bars to naturalization. | Yes |

*Source:* Adapted with author's modifications from Patrick Weil, "Access to Citizenship: A Comparison of Twenty-Five Nationality Laws," in *Citizenship Today: Global Perspectives and Practices,* ed. T. Alexander Aleinikoff and Douglas Klusmeyer (Washington, D.C.: Carnegie Endowment for International Peace, 2001), pp. 22–3.

In the pursuit of legitimate goals, we believe that states may reasonably require some period of residence, knowledge of the language, and absence of a criminal record. We discuss each of these in turn.

Table 1 shows that five years is the median period of residence required by states before naturalization. We recommend that states that require a longer period reduce it to five years. Five years is a reasonable period of time for the immigrant to acquire the different elements of socialization. The requirement of residence means physical presence. Temporary absences from the country should not be an obstacle to the accumulation of the required number of years of residence.

Nearly all states' laws include provisions to facilitate or accelerate the naturalization of foreigners married to citizens (see table 2). A majority of countries provide a reduction of the period of residence for spouses. We recommend that such provisions be extended to same sex couples in those states that recognize same sex contracts or unions.

Requirements regarding language acquisition, while permissible, ought to be related to the situation of the applicant. For example, in France, instructions and court decisions require officials to take into account the circumstances of the applicant in evaluating his or her level of French proficiency. In the United States, the language requirement may be waived for elderly applicants who are long-term residents. Written tests are generally preferable to oral ones, and standardized answers preferable to ones requiring subjective evaluation.

Absence of a criminal record is a legitimate requirement, but a criminal record should not be a permanent barrier to citizenship where it is not grounds for deportation. If a state permits an immigrant to permanently reside in the society after a criminal conviction, it should also permit that person to apply for naturalization. Criminal conviction may be a valid basis for extending the normal residency requirement (for example, by not counting time spent in jail or on probation toward satisfying a residency requirement), but rules regarding extensions should also include ameliorative provisions that take into account family links and evidence of effective reintegration in the society.

*Acceptable Supplemental Criteria.*    In addition to these basic criteria, some states include knowledge of history and culture requirements. Many also charge fees. As to these conditions, we make the following recommendations.

As with language requirements, written exams that test knowledge of the history or culture are generally preferable to oral ones; and standardized answers are preferable to ones requiring subjective evaluation. Here also the standards themselves ought to be related to the circumstances of the applicant. More

Table 2. *Effect of Marriage on Naturalization in Selected Countries*

| Country | Existence of a Specific Provision | Residence | Delay | Other Requirements |
|---|---|---|---|---|
| Australia | No | — | — | — |
| Austria | Yes | 4 years (if married 1 year) 3 years (if married 2 years) | — | — |
| Belgium | Yes | 3 years | — | — |
| Canada | No | — | — | — |
| Denmark | No | — | — | — |
| Estonia | No | — | — | — |
| Finland | Yes | 3 years | 2 years | — |
| France | Yes | — | 1 year | Facilitated naturalization (by declaration) |
| Germany | Yes | 5 years | — | — |
| Greece | No | — | — | — |
| Ireland | Yes | — | 3 years | — |
| Israel | Yes | — | — | At discretion of Minister of Interior, no commission of certain crimes |
| Italy | Yes | 6 months in Italy or total 3 years abroad | — | — |
| Latvia | No | — | — | — |
| Lithuania | No | — | — | — |
| Luxembourg | Yes | 3 years | — | Proof of life in common |
| Mexico | Yes | 2 years | — | — |
| The Netherlands | Yes | 3 years | — | — |
| Portugal | Yes | 3 years | — | — |
| Russia | Yes | — | — | Facilitated naturalization |
| South Africa | Yes | — | 2 years | — |
| Spain | Yes | — | 1 year | — |
| Sweden | Yes | Permanent (3 years) | 2 years | — |
| United Kingdom | Yes | 3 years | — | — |
| United States | Yes | 3 years | — | Same as for other aliens |

Source: Patrick Weil, "Access to Citizenship: A Comparison of Twenty-Five Nationality Laws," in *Citizenship Today: Global Perspectives and Practices*, ed. T. Alexander Aleinikoff and Douglas Klusmeyer (Washington, D.C.: Carnegie Endowment for International Peace, 2001), p. 24.

modest standards or exemptions might also pertain to applicants who have lived in the society for a considerable period of time.

The majority of states require fees for naturalization. Fees may help states pay for the cost of naturalization procedures, but they should not be set at a level that they deter access to citizenship. Some states accomplish this by permitting fee waivers for applicants with reduced means.

*Conditions That Should Be Avoided.*   Conditions requiring that applicants have economic resources and be of personal good character are included in many naturalization laws. We think such conditions should be avoided.

From a contemporary democratic perspective, tying citizenship to the economic resources of the applicant seems inappropriate and a throwback to an earlier, class-biased conception of democracy. We do not believe the consideration of sufficient income—or economic status—is an acceptable criterion.

General, open-ended clauses about "good moral character" or "evidence of integration with society" provide officials a great deal of discretion to reject individual persons on wholly subjective or otherwise arbitrary grounds. This problem remains a concern even when courts have narrowed the discretionary authority of officials in interpreting such clauses. We consider these to contradict the requirement for a clear, limited, precise, and objective procedure.

*Resources for Naturalization.*   In many states, naturalization services suffer from high neglect in the distribution of the state budget—perhaps in part because foreign residents are not voters. This lack of priority has led to backlogs of months and even years. Applicants are entitled to timely processing of their cases. Naturalization is not only in the interest of the immigrant. A policy that transforms a foreigner into a full citizen is of significant public and national interest and therefore deserves a high priority in public policy.

### Summary of Recommendations

Our analysis has led us to make the following conclusions and recommendations:

*Second and Third Generations*

For *jus soli* states:
- Foreign-born minor children of lawful immigrants who have received significant social or educational formation in the receiving country should be entitled to citizenship. More precisely, those who, as children, (1) have

received six years of schooling or (2) have spent ten years of residence in the country satisfy this criterion.

For states without a *jus soli* provision:
- Members of the third generation should be automatically entitled to citizenship at birth.
- Members of the second generation should be entitled to citizenship if they are born on the national territory and either they or one of their parents lawfully resides there.
- Foreign-born children of lawful immigrants should be entitled to citizenship under the terms recommended for *jus soli* states.

*First Generation*

- Criteria for naturalization should be clear, limited, precise, and objective. Administrative discretion should be delimited and subject to judicial review.
- States may reasonably require a period of residence, knowledge of the language, and take into account a criminal record.
- A required period of residence should not exceed five years.
- Language requirements should be related to the circumstances of the applicant.
- A criminal record should not be a permanent barrier to citizenship where it is not grounds for deportation.
- If knowledge of history or culture is required, the standards should be related to circumstances of the applicant.
- A naturalization fee should not deter access to citizenship. Individuals lacking adequate resources should be exempted from the fee for naturalization.
- Conditions requiring resources and personal good character should be avoided.
- Adequate resources should be devoted to naturalization services.

# CHAPTER TWO

# Managing Dual Nationality

IN TODAY'S WORLD, dual citizenship is increasingly common, despite a global legal order nominally hostile to such a status. Because that hostility is increasingly at odds with the needs and realities of an interconnected globe linked by rapidly improving communications, transport, and commerce, dual citizenship has widely but unevenly eroded. New practices that tolerate or foster dual nationality, however, have often sprung up without close scrutiny or without systematic attention to the full implications of changed practices. Such inattention may have been understandable when dual nationality was rare and effectively opposed by states. But dual nationality is no longer an aberrant occurrence, to be tolerated in the shadows or handled in the deep recesses of bureaucracies. The old arguments against the status no longer hold the same force they may have had a hundred years ago. But many of those arguments do address points of genuine concern that should not be wholly lost from sight in the new conditions.

We conclude that the old stance against dual nationality is no longer appropriate. Dual nationality should now be straightforwardly accepted when it is the product of individual choice (including choice by one's parents) and reflects genuine links with both of the states concerned, but it should be regulated and managed through a more consistent body of practice worldwide. To this end, we develop recommendations for new global rules or principles both more appropriate to the current realities and more mindful of historic concerns about dual nationality.

### Growth of Dual Nationality

The world community entered the last third of the twentieth century with a domestic and international legal order that generally treated dual nationality as unnatural and undesirable. Whether this attitude derived from conceptual logic—postulating national loyalties as exclusive and indivisible—or from concerns about practical difficulties in the realms of diplomatic protection, civil status, military service, or taxation, it was nonetheless widely shared. The Hague Convention of 1930 begins with an oft-quoted preamble that prescribes: "[E]very person should have a nationality and should have one nationality only" (League of Nations 1930: 89). Court decisions have frequently spoken of the evils or dilemmas inherent in dual nationality but without elaborate argumentation in support of that conclusion.[11] Even the Council of Europe, little more than a decade after adopting the European Convention on Human Rights, proceeded to adopt a 1963 Convention designed to reduce the incidence of multiple nationality, seeing no tension between the freedoms of the former and the restrictions of the latter (United Nations 1963: 221). National laws also reflected this hostile stance—most prominently in widespread requirements (in the laws of both immigration and emigration countries) that forced a person taking up the citizenship of a new country through naturalization to surrender all other allegiances.

Despite this legal framework, the last several decades have witnessed a significant proliferation of dual or multiple nationality (Feldblum 2000: 475, 478). The principal reason is by now treated as commonplace: The world has become progressively more interconnected through new technologies that greatly facilitate communications, travel, and commerce and through political changes that are increasingly receptive to cross-border trade and investment. More and more people, at all levels of the economic and social ladder, now live, for a time at least, outside their countries of origin. Cross-national marriages have proliferated, and the offspring in such cases usually obtain both parents' nationalities *jure sanguinis*. Even among couples of the same nationality, more births occur outside the national territory. If the country of birth observes the *jus soli* rule for transmission of citizenship, the child then typically gains multiple nationality. Lengthy residence also often results in permanent settlement in a new country, bringing with it inducements to consider seriously the option of naturalization, despite continuing ties to the country of origin.

In this climate, many countries have changed their laws to accommodate dual nationality. The Council of Europe, source of the 1963 convention explicitly designed to limit the incidence of multiple citizenship, adopted several protocols that greatly softened the restrictive message, and in 1997 it accepted a new European Convention on Nationality that readily accepts dual nationality and attempts in modest but important ways to regulate it (Council of Europe 1997, 1993).[12] Moreover, a growing literature is not content with merely advocating tolerance of dual nationality; many writers strongly support its expansion as a means of fostering global peace, enhancing international trade, spreading democratic values, and observing human rights.

### Legal Tools Capable of Limiting Dual Nationality and Their Limits

The legal order would not have been powerless to avoid a proliferation of dual nationality even in the teeth of increasing global commerce and migration. But the failure to deploy available legal tools effectively for that nominally shared purpose testifies strongly to the deep-rootedness of multiple citizenships in the world of the twenty-first century. Those tools, and their relative ineffectiveness in recent decades, merit a brief review.

#### Limiting Dual Nationality at Birth

If all states allowed transmission of citizenship only by descent, *jus sanguinis,* then dual nationality would certainly be reduced in the case of children born outside their parents' country of nationality. (Uniform adoption of *jus soli* as the basis for transmission of citizenship would equally—or perhaps more effectively—reduce the incidence of dual nationality, but *jus soli* has been less widely accepted, and no country in the modern world uses it as the only basis for attribution of citizenship.) No such global uniformity has been seriously considered, however, even at the high point of support for the one-nationality-only principle. The major countries of immigration have generally favored strong *jus soli* rules, while most countries of emigration adopt *jus sanguinis* regimes— despite their nominal opposition to dual nationality. In this setting, dual nationality inevitably proliferates as the global economy and cheaper transportation result in more family migration.

In any event, as noted in chapter one, sole reliance on *jus sanguinis* has proven increasingly undesirable, particularly in situations where families take up permanent residence elsewhere. Second or third generations are born in the new country and remain technically foreigners. Even some governments committed to the notion that their countries are not countries of immigration have come to regret or oppose a situation where such children lack the nationality of the only country whose life they have known. The most graphic recent example of the power of this trend may be found in Germany. Despite the nation's historic commitment to *jus sanguinis* and strong public opposition to dual nationality, in 1999 Germany amended its laws to provide citizenship to children born in its territory of foreign parents who had been resident for eight years.[13] In short, insistence on transmission solely by way of *jus sanguinis* appears to be a durably workable policy only if the state is rigorous in preventing immigration or in insisting that foreigners must not settle but must leave after a temporary stay, even of several years' duration. Democratic states have found this rigor virtually impossible to enforce, owing either to political realities or to legal restrictions found in constitution or treaty. When immigrant families settle in for generations, states find that they need either *jus soli* rules or eased naturalization (often including acceptance that the new citizen will retain the former national affiliation as well) to facilitate integration and to avoid the creation of a permanently estranged class of lifelong residents.

Finally, even if uniform application of *jus sanguinis* could somehow be achieved, the incidence of dual nationality would still expand because of increasing numbers of cross-national marriages.[14] Of course, the legal cupboard is not bare for those states that might have wanted to avoid dual nationality even in these circumstances. In the early twentieth century, in fact, most states had an answer for this perceived problem. Their legal rules provided for the child to receive the citizenship only of the father—and they often virtually forced the wife to surrender her previous nationality and take on the citizenship of her husband as well, whatever her wishes.

This legal regime clearly minimized dual nationality and helped assure that families shared the same formal citizenship status, but at the cost of blatant gender discrimination and the thwarting of the will of many married women. As a result, such laws were an early target of the women's suffrage movement, and they began to disappear rather promptly in a great many countries after women achieved the right to vote. By the latter third of the twentieth century, nearly all such discriminatory laws had been repealed in democratic states, with the result that most children of mixed marriages obtained the citizenship of both parents.[15] Indeed, the movement toward gender equality has been a major contributor to the increasing incidence of dual nationality. Because it is inconceivable that modern democracies will return to the old discriminatory laws, and because cross-national marriages are bound to increase as a result of growing travel, study, and work in foreign lands, this source of dual nationality will expand.

## Election Requirements

States of course could still enforce eventual mono-nationality of those who acquire dual nationality at birth, through a requirement that the dual national choose or, in the common phrase, "elect," a single nationality at the age of majority. Many states have had this requirement at times, but its use has been declining. Its support has been uneven at best, even in the heyday of the opposition to dual nationality. (The Hague Convention of 1930 contained no election requirement.) Nonetheless some states still impose an election requirement on dual citizens when they reach the age of majority. And that the idea of a required election of citizenship still has some life is evidenced in its inclusion in Germany's 1999 liberalizing legislation. Children who at birth obtain both German citizenship under the new *jus soli* rules as well as the citizenship of their parents' country of origin are supposed to choose one nationality or the other at the age of majority. This policy will not face a full test until 2013, the deadline by which the first such elections must take place; it is an open question whether its constitutionality will be upheld by German courts. In any event, the tide in Europe is flowing more broadly against such an imposition. Not long before Germany enacted this law, the Council of Europe adopted a provision in its 1997 convention on nationality that would seem to forbid imposing a required election on children in these circumstances.[16]

### Restricting Dual Nationality at Time of Naturalization

Legal regimes often formally require the loss or renunciation of all other nationalities at the time of naturalization. In the 1960s, the codes of the major democracies generally contained such a restriction. But over time most receiving countries applied these provisions with decreasing rigor. For example, many such codes contained exceptions to the renunciation requirement (such as, when the country of initial nationality makes it difficult or prohibitively costly to secure release from its citizenship) that were intended originally for narrow application. In recent decades, these exceptions came to be applied with increasing liberality—as happened in Germany and the Netherlands, to use two notable examples (Koslowski 1998: 734, 744). Elsewhere, the requirement of renunciation became something of an empty verbal gesture. The United States, for example, retains by statute its formal requirement, as part of the naturalization oath, that new citizens renounce all prior allegiances. But the U.S. Department of State now treats this provision as essentially unenforceable, sometimes advising prospective new citizens not to worry about plans to continue exercising the rights and privileges of the original nationality. This stance is rationalized by a judgment that the renunciatory language in the U.S. naturalization oath would not be regarded by most other countries as effectively terminating their nationality. And the statutes of many countries have explicitly come to accept dual nationality on the part of naturalizing immigrants, notably including other countries with significant levels of immigration, such as Australia, Canada, and France.[17]

A similar—and perhaps even more striking—shift in attitude toward naturalization can be discerned on the part of countries of recent emigration. Traditionally many tended to regard their nationals who took up full citizenship elsewhere as virtual traitors who could not be allowed to retain their original nationality. But by the 1990s, many key emigration countries moved to the opposite stance, enacting laws to facilitate retention of the original nationality despite naturalization elsewhere (Freeman and Ögelman 1998; Jones-Correa 2000). For example, El Salvador made this change in 1983, the Dominican Republic in 1994, and Mexico in 1998. Several Eastern and Central European states made the same shift when they adopted new nationality laws in the wake of the major political changes in 1989 to 1990 (Leibich 2000: 103–5). Hence naturalization increasingly leaves the naturalized member of the new polity as a dual national—a status tolerated or even encouraged by one or both of the states involved. But several key states have not made these changes, and in others the continuation of a renunciation requirement, even if often waived or treated as ineffective, sends a confusing signal to those considering naturalization. (For more on the effect of naturalization upon retention of original nationality, see table 3.)

### Assessing the Case For and Against Dual Nationality

The historical developments recounted above strongly suggest that dual nationality will continue to proliferate in a world of increasing mobility and interconnectedness. It also reveals that the trend is not wholly beyond the capacity of nations to counteract. But should they do so? This section examines the principal arguments against dual nationality. We conclude that either they are unpersuasive in the conditions of the twenty-first century, or their underlying concerns could be better addressed through less restrictive measures that are more consistent with the basic principles of liberal democracies.

In general, it is important to recognize here that most of the concerns raised about dual nationality rest on normative inferences and hypothetical conjectures rather than on empirically documented or quantifiable case examples. The near absence of such evidence put forward by opponents of dual nationality is telling, because its rising incidence is hardly a new phenomenon. Pointing to isolated examples or offering anecdotal accounts does not qualify as evidence of a pattern or a trend. Presumably, if the opponents are right, there should be a demonstrable correspondence between the rising incidence of dual

Table 3.  *Effect of Naturalization on Retention of Original Nationality: Rules of Selected Countries*

| Country | Required to Renounce or Surrender Foreign Nationality upon Naturalization | Lose Nationality upon Foreign Naturalization |
|---|---|---|
| Argentina | Yes | Yes |
| Australia | No | Yes |
| Austria | Yes | Yes |
| Canada | No | No |
| Denmark | Yes | Yes |
| Ecuador | No | No |
| El Salvador | No | No |
| Estonia | Yes | No |
| Finland | Yes | Yes |
| France | No | No |
| Germany | Yes | No |
| Israel | Yes (does not apply to Jews, under the Law of Return) | No |
| Japan | Yes | No |
| Lithuania | Yes | Yes |
| Mexico | Yes | No |
| Portugal | No | No |
| Russian Federation | No | No |
| South Africa | No | Yes |
| Spain | Yes (with exception for nationals of Hispanic American countries) | Yes (with exception for nationals of Hispanic American countries) |
| Sweden | Yes | Yes |
| Turkey | No | No (assuming permission of Turkish government, regularly granted) |
| United Kingdom | No | No |
| United States | Yes | No |

*Notes:* "No" indicates a stance favorable to dual or multiple nationality in connection with naturalization.

The chart indicates the basic or general rule in each system, as set forth in constitution, statute, or regulation. Many countries recognize exceptions or qualifications in a bewildering variety of forms, and some are more tolerant in practice of dual nationality upon naturalization than the formal provisions would seem to allow. Exceptions or qualifications are noted in the chart only where the exception or qualification applies to a high percentage of covered persons or is otherwise especially significant.

The column dealing with foreign naturalizations sets forth the consequences that flow from naturalization upon the individual's own voluntary application; therefore it does not deal with acquisition of nationality by operation of law, as upon marriage or the naturalization of a minor child's parents.

nationality and the kind of systematic problems that these opponents predict. We might expect to find such a pattern of correspondence in the experience of major receiving states over the last century, but no such pattern has ever been shown.

Nonetheless, we believe that the arguments against dual nationality merit careful consideration because they still resonate with the public in many nations' debates on this topic and because they raise issues that need to be taken into account in the policy management of dual nationality. After a century in which the incidence of dual nationality has steadily risen, however, the key question is no longer whether this development is good or bad, but rather how can states best structure policies that minimize potential problems and advance other important objectives.

### Arguments Against Dual Nationality

*Loyalty.* Opponents of dual nationality often treat national allegiance as inherently exclusive and indivisible. In this concept, dual nationality is viewed as analogous to bigamy, amounting to a kind of cheating on both polities.

Whatever force this argument might have had in the eighteenth- or nineteenth-century world order—when sovereignty was often vested in jealous monarchs, transnational interaction was limited, and the state system was characterized as a kind of international anarchy—it carries far less heft today. For a nation to claim exclusive and absolutely paramount loyalty is the hallmark of totalitarianism. Liberal democratic principles, in contrast, accord great latitude to individuals in choosing their values and commitments. Empirically, modern nations in overwhelming proportions tolerate or encourage a wide range of competing loyalties and affiliations in civil society—to family, business, local community, religious denominations, sports teams, nongovernmental organizations promoting both political and nonpolitical causes—and do not treat such allegiances (even when they have an international dimension) as bigamous or as incompatible with a healthy level of loyalty to the nation-state.

Dual nationals also may feel strong ties to two nation-states without ordinarily sensing that the commitment to one compromises or clashes with their loyalty to the other. For one reason, nations are increasingly bound by common, or at least harmonious, policies and objectives—given the growing acceptance of democratic principles, of internationally recognized human rights, and of some form of a market economy. Moreover, wars between nation-states— once the ultimate test for a citizen's loyalties—have grown increasingly rare. Armed conflict in today's world is far more likely within a nation-state. In fact, many cross-border military interventions in the past decade have not been state-based but have been taken instead under the auspices of international organizations or regional alliances. The end of the Cold War has improved the odds of continued international peace, and the expanding linkage of states in regional or global organizations helps promote compatible policies. As more decision making occurs at the transnational level, in any case, the very concept of exclusive political loyalty becomes more problematic.

This is not to say that allegiance to the nation is unimportant. In fact, the contrary is true. It calls forth the engagement in politics that democracies need, and a healthy measure of civic loyalty helps dampen temptations for violent opposition or secession that could be felt whenever one faction is outvoted on issues about which people care deeply. Some observers believe that only a developed sense of civic nationalism offers hope to counter tendencies toward social divisiveness, whether based on nationalism, class, religion, or other factors. Therefore, any real devaluation of citizenship in this active sense that would undercut civic solidarity would be a legitimate concern. But the needed level of loyalty or commitment to a democratic polity of which one is a member is certainly possible in the modern world even if one holds two or more nationalities. Indeed, loyalty is likely to be far stronger to the state in which one maintains a thickening web of local connections, such as owning property, investing in a business, building a career, or schooling oneself or one's children.

Finally, this kind of argument against dual nationality can be a proxy for opposing the full acceptance of new members on other grounds. Receiving states that wish to discourage permanent settlement and naturalization of persons deemed undesirable for religious, racial, or other cultural reasons can invoke the formal principle of mono-nationality as a culturally neutral rationale. To the extent that the acquisition of a new nationality is understood as a renunciation of all-important attachments associated with a former homeland, the principle of mono-nationality becomes an effective deterrent to naturalizing for many who retain such attachments. In today's world, liberal-democratic states are increasingly reluctant to acknowledge openly any exclusions or discrimination predicated on ascriptive criteria, such as religion and race. The principle of mono-nationality offers the decided advantage of basing unfavorable treatment on a more defensible pretext.

*Exit Option.* Dual nationals have an option that most others within the nation's citizenry do not enjoy, owing to the modern world's developed web of immigration controls: Dual nationals have another country to which they can readily emigrate if conditions in the first deteriorate radically. The concern is that this option may foster less than responsible exercise of their duties—in particular, it might incline dual nationals toward the radical extremes of politics. If extremist positions gain ascendancy and provoke economic disaster, widespread corruption, or violence, this objection runs, then dual nationals can simply retreat to their other home states.

Although there may be some force to this concern, it probably exaggerates the effect of dual nationality, and in any event it can be curbed through lesser measures than a ban on the status. First, despite modern immigration controls, mono-nationals at the higher end of the economic ladder in fact often enjoy opportunities to relocate elsewhere if conditions in their country of nationality deteriorate, yet this fact is not taken as a basis for denying them participation in their state's government. Indeed, regional arrangements like the EU have eliminated legal barriers to the exit option for nationals of the participating states, without arousing deep fears about irresponsible voting. Second, physical migration and resettlement do not constitute so ready an option as economists' models presume. Guest workers in the 1950s through the 1970s widely reported on surveys that they intended to return to their countries of origin after a few years enjoying the economic benefits in a foreign country—but surprisingly high proportions remained in the countries to which their families had grown accustomed, even if they lacked citizenship and suffered other forms of discrimination there. Inertia and familiarity often keep people rooted despite adverse surrounding conditions and theoretical options of alternative residence.

*Double Voting and Unfairness.* Citizenship is often viewed as the quintessential marker or framework for equality in democratic societies. Whatever disparities exist in class, education, talent, or economic position, as a citizen each person counts equally. Dual nationals, it might be argued, have achieved a status superior to their fellow citizens because they can vote in two polities.

As a conceptual matter, however, the principle of one person/one vote is not violated if a person casts two votes in elections in two independent states. These separate votes are not aggregated in electing representatives or deciding issues and are therefore not given a higher weight than the votes of persons who hold only one nationality. The relevant arena for applying the principle of one person/one vote is therefore usually a single nation's politics. Dual nationality wins no privileges here. Further, on a practical level, many obstacles exist to the simultaneous exercise of the franchise in two separate states. Each state sets its own voting rules, and such regulatory schemes cover an extraordinarily wide range with regard to voting by nonresident citizens. Some ban such voting altogether, even by mono-nationals resident outside the territory. At the opposite pole, some states have special parliamentary seats for representatives of those who live abroad. For those states that do allow nonresident voting, with or without special forms of representation, further variety exists. Some allow absentee voting by mail, while others make arrangements through their consulates, and specific practices can make any such distant franchise easier or more difficult to exercise. In virtually every situation, however, voting participation by those who live outside national territory has been quite low. In these circumstances, the practical impact of dual nationals' double voting is insignificant.

*Instructed Voting.* Some opposition to dual nationality stems from a concern that dual nationals may vote as instructed by the leaders of the other state, rather than as an authentic exercise of their own will in judging what is best for the sovereign people of the state in which the election is occurring. Indiscreet comments by government officials in countries of emigration, particularly during the time when such countries were changing their laws to encourage its nonresidents to naturalize elsewhere, have sometimes fed these concerns.

Nonetheless, no evidence exists of successful commands of this sort by countries of emigration. And even if one could identify such occurrences, a ban on dual nationality would hardly provide an effective barrier. Citizens are entitled to make up their own minds about what policies are best, and they need not follow some official version of the national interests as propounded by the state holding the vote. That their judgments may coincide with arguments or even words framed as commands by foreign leaders does not prove the illegitimacy of the voter's choice.

Lifelong mono-nationals may develop an affinity for another country, whether inspired by work assignments or tourist visits there, that country's literature or cuisine, or adherence to its religion or secular philosophy. Even if such affection seems to guide their choices in the voting booth, they are not thereby disqualified from voting. Perhaps it is true that persons who once held the nationality of another state are more susceptible to such influences. But if so, requiring formal renunciation at the time of naturalization seems unlikely to negate them. Such influences have probably been operative in this setting even when loss of the other state's nationality was more strictly enforced at the time of naturalization. If a state is insistent on preventing such affinities, banning dual nationality is a paltry step. The government would have to be far more rigorous in banning international travel, commerce, study, and immigration than virtually any state is now willing to be. In short, in the modern world, cross-national travel, business, and migration are likely to generate these sorts of influences and affinities.

*Cultural Nation.* Opposition to dual nationality sometimes stems from concerns about unwanted changes to revered practices or beliefs, changes that are attributed to the growing ranks of newcomers living in a society. Such opposition, however, often presumes a preexisting cultural homogeneity that is exceedingly rare in the modern world. It also underestimates the degree to which national cultures are subject to change, divergent interpretations, and internal dissent. In any event, to the extent that such changes in valued cultural elements occur, little of the blame can be laid at the feet of dual nationality. The very presence of significant populations from other countries is bound to have some cultural impact, at least in the absence of rigorous control measures imposed on only a subset of residents—measures that would probably be incompatible with a democratic society. More than dual citizenship, then, immigration is the truly responsible agent here. In any case, modern communications—including satellite television transmissions, e-mail, and the Internet—make it highly unlikely that cultures can be insulated even if migration is tightly controlled. For better or worse, cultural influences have globalized, and resistance to unwanted changes will have to be based primarily on the inherent strength and appeal of the challenged cultural practice.

*Diplomatic Protection.* Historically, complications in the exercise of diplomatic protection for a state's nationals residing or traveling abroad have been invoked against the acceptance or recognition of dual nationality. But this concern has often been misplaced, as it does not necessarily result from dual nationality, properly understood. Many such celebrated controversies, dating from the nineteenth century, stemmed from the now discredited concept of perpetual allegiance, as practiced by the country of initial nationality. The individuals in question believed they had naturalized in a second country and thereby had shed the initial country's citizenship, but the first state still regarded them as its nationals.

When the individual in question truly does hold dual nationality, international law already provides rules to minimize conflict. Through much of the past century, a country was generally considered disentitled to exercise diplomatic protection against another country whose nationality the individual held. Any country of nationality, in other words, could apply its own laws of whatever character to its own citizens, whether mono-nationals or multiple nationals, and was immune to diplomatic protest from other states.

This rule, disabling diplomatic protection against any country of which the person holds nationality, may be insufficiently protective for today's world, but the practice was never uniform, and in any case this rule has considerably eroded. Some treaties have provided explicitly for determining the dominant or effective nationality in such circumstances (it is usually that of the country of primary residence), and they often permit the identified state to protect its citizen even against the other country of nationality.[18] Some international panels and tribunals, including the Iran-U.S. Claims Tribunal, have also adopted such a practice without explicit treaty foundation; they permit the country of dominant and effective nationality to put forward a claim on behalf of a dual national, even though the person is also a citizen of the allegedly violating state.

Beyond this, protection of an individual's rights can now be based as well on a wholly different and more universal foundation than the classic doctrines of diplomatic protection, which (as has often been lamented) were wholly agnostic about a nation's treatment of its own nationals. Today, protecting states can lodge protests (and sometimes take far stronger actions) based on a violation of international human rights, even if the only victims are lifelong mononationals of the allegedly violating state. In a world order that increasingly, and commendably, accepts this broad understanding of universal human rights as a possible basis for interstate complaint or contention, difficulties of diplomatic protection cannot seriously be maintained as a significant objection to dual nationality.

*Military Service and Conscription.*    In the more anarchic world of the nineteenth and early twentieth century, when classic state-versus-state war was a more available instrument of national power, and when abrupt changes in alliances often meant that yesterday's ally became today's enemy, suspicion about dual nationals among the members of a nation's military was understandable. However much one could tolerate complex and layered loyalties in times of peace, an outright shooting war was seen to demand unquestioning obedience.

The world order has changed considerably since then, particularly with the end of the Cold War. A widening circle of democratic nations has made enduring alliances based on genuinely shared values and interests, far more durable than monarchs' temporary judgments of advantage. The economies and even military forces of some nations are so closely linked as to make disentanglement nearly inconceivable. Even most nondemocratic nations participate in a UN system that has helped curb international war and often provides the forum for minimizing the violence or the cross-border impact of internal wars. Many nations have abolished conscription. Of those that still conscript, many have entered into bilateral or multilateral treaties that protect a dual national against multiple requirements of military service. These usually give primacy to the claim of the state of residence and provide that service in one state of nationality discharges the obligation in the second state, at least short of emergency or general mobilization (League of Nations 1930; United Nations 1963; Council of Europe 1997).[19] In any case, the prospect of the ultimate challenge to dual nationals' loyalties—war between their two countries—has been rendered far less likely. Concern about conflicting military obligations no longer provides a convincing rationale for rigid rules absolutely banning dual citizenship.

But the concern has not disappeared altogether. International wars do sometimes still occur, and nothing guarantees that the trend toward peaceful resolution of disputes is irreversible, even among currently friendly states. As a result states may validly restrict mono-nationals' access to sensitive positions critical to national security. In times of sharp international conflict, nations may be entitled to impose certain choices on dual nationals who wish to serve in their militaries, perhaps including renunciation of citizenship in hostile states. In any event, at such times a clearly available mechanism for relinquishing one nationality would also be in the interest of the individuals affected, because those who hold dual nationality in two openly hostile nations run the risk that their actions in support of one would be regarded as treason by the other country.[20]

This possibility, plus the risk of conscription in a state wherein the person does not reside, illustrates a broader point: Dual nationality is not invariably in the interest of the persons holding such a status. Hence some mechanism for voluntary expatriation, with only minimal qualifications, should be preserved.

*Conflict of Laws Regarding Civil Status, Inheritance, Taxation, and Similar Issues.* Many states, particularly in the civil law tradition, base certain key private-law determinations—including marital status, adoption, other family obligations, and inheritance—on the nationality of the affected individual. When a person holds multiple nationalities, conflicting or irreconcilable rules may formally apply. Taxation regimes may also conflict, or at least compound the burdens of dual nationals, because some states, notably including the United States, assert the right to tax their citizens wherever resident. Similar multiple regulatory claims may be made on the basis of citizenship, even when citizens act or reside outside the national territory.

Although these multiple confusions are sometimes invoked as a reason to resist dual nationality, they fall far short of providing decisive arguments against the status. Other methods of deciding a dispute when potentially applicable laws conflict are certainly available, primarily by giving primacy to the law of the state with which dual nationals have their primary contacts—ordinarily the state of habitual residence. Such choice-of-law provisions may be adopted in national law or coordinated through treaty. Resolving these questions by treaty carries many advantages, including the chance to adopt more detailed criteria so as to minimize disputes over identifying the state with principal contacts. Similarly, numerous states have bilateral or multilateral treaties avoiding or minimizing multiple tax liabilities (as applied to all who are subject to taxation by the states concerned, not only dual nationals), usually by providing an offset against tax liabilities for payments made to another contracting state. Where such provisions do not exist, dual nationals should probably be deemed to have chosen the extra burdens (at least so long as some reasonable avenue of expatriation remains available).

But these alternative ways of resolving questions of civil status carry one further disadvantage. They can conceivably leave different rules applying at different times to members of the same family unit, depending on where the members reside, whether all members of the family have taken on the same citizenship, or other factors. Such a divergence of treatment within a single family may be unavoidable in a mobile world, but it is not necessarily desirable. The regime of a hundred years ago, which imposed a single membership on all members of the nuclear family, was problematic not because of its aim to give the family a common status, but because of its discriminatory means, uniformly submerging the identity and allegiance of the wife. States may properly seek to promote a similar unity of family membership today, without the discrimination. Many states have done so in modest ways, in addition to the increasing recognition of dual nationality—for example through measures that accelerate the acquisition by spouses and children of the nationality of the other adult member of the family, or policies that ease the relinquishment of a former nationality by those who choose to retain only the nationality of the spouse.

### Arguments for Recognizing Dual Nationality

We have already described the extent to which the phenomenon of dual nationality is an integral product of the modern international system. There also good reasons for states to adopt a tolerant, if not permissive, stance toward dual nationality as a matter in its own right. We summarize briefly several of these reasons here.

*Reflecting Deeply Felt Affiliations, Connections, and Loyalties.*    In our increasingly interconnected world, many people live outside the country of their birth or are born in nations different from where their parents were born. Many regard links with both those countries (through family, property, business ties, culture, religion) as important, vital, worthy of nurture, and perhaps even foundational to their identities. In wishing to deepen their ties with one of the countries, they neither wish to, nor see the need of, casting off completely their links to the other country. A commitment to respecting pluralist differences, whether cultural, political, or social, is fundamental to modern democratic principles. This respect applies to those same differences expressed by nationality.

*Promoting Naturalization and Integration.* Lengthy lawful residence outside the country of one's nationality has grown increasingly common. States experiencing this phenomenon have come to appreciate the importance of promoting the civic, political, and social integration of long-term residents. Often naturalization rules that require the surrender of the original nationality stand as an obstacle, either in fact or in perception, to achieving this goal. (The effect can be compounded if the original country of nationality limits inheritance or property rights for nonnationals.) Accepting dual nationality on the part of citizens who naturalize can contribute toward improved integration and a healthier level of identification with the country of residence.

*Facilitating Free Movement Between States.* Some long-time residents in a foreign state, though eligible for naturalization there, have been reluctant to take up that citizenship if the laws of either state required surrender of the original nationality, for a very pragmatic reason not wholly captured in argument. They are concerned that they could not then move freely back and forth between the two states with which they have links because they would become subject to the varying qualifications for admission of noncitizens in the country of their birth. This concern was of lesser significance in earlier eras, when transportation was so arduous and expensive that return travel would be seen only as a remote and unlikely—and certainly infrequent—contingency. Today, both business connections and family needs may dictate frequent migration and the continuation of close ties despite long distances. The assurance of admission that dual citizenship can afford is therefore more significant.

*Promoting Inclusiveness.* Although democratic polities have a long history of exclusionary practices, most of these practices are now widely understood to be incompatible with modern liberal-democratic principles. One such core principle is that the governed have a fundamental right to representation; this right is guaranteed through basic citizenship. Prohibitions on dual nationality have the effect of disenfranchising large numbers of permanent legal residents who forgo naturalization merely because they seek to retain another formal nationality. One may say that this is a self-inflicted wound and that a state has a right to insist that its citizenship be exclusive of all others. But when it is recognized that the arguments against dual nationality are relatively weak, then such conditions on rights to participate in governance begin to appear unjustified under liberal-democratic principles.

## Recommendations

Our central premise is this: In the conditions of the modern world, dual nationality often reflects the reality of complex loyalties and allegiances in an increasingly interconnected world, marked by a growing circle of democratic states with converging interests. The status should no longer be suppressed. Instead, it should be explicitly accepted and managed more thoughtfully than it was in a world order that largely pretended either that it did not exist or that it was a temporary aberration not worthy of nuanced regulation. With this central premise in mind, we offer the following specific guiding principles.

### Accept Dual or Multiple Nationality for Individuals with a Genuine Link to the Countries Concerned

Such multiple links can result from cross-national marriage, birth within a country that is not the country of the parents' nationality, naturalization in a country where the person has been resident for a period of years, relocation to the country of a parent's nationality, and certain other circumstances. States should honor individual choices to nurture those linkages through dual nationality, and, within certain broad limits sketched in later recommendations, respect and empower such individual decisions. This change should carry the additional advantage of encouraging long-resident immigrants to take the citizenship of their new country. It would also send the important message—to new citizens and old—that full membership entails not only economic arrangements (which may have been the immigrants' primary link theretofore) but also political engagement. Specifically, we recommend that:

(1) *States should therefore explicitly repeal legal provisions that require the renunciation of former nationalities upon naturalization or that impose the loss of nationality on citizens who naturalize elsewhere.* It is not sufficient simply to disregard them in practice or to apply liberal exceptions, because this sends confusing signals to those contemplating naturalization and may deter that outcome even where the state does not so intend. Nevertheless, it certainly would be appropriate for states that so wish to require an oath of allegiance as part of the naturalization requirements.

(2) *States should sustain gender-neutral rules that allow children generally to inherit the nationality of both parents.*

(3) *States should not require dual-nationality children to choose among nationalities upon attaining majority.*

(4) *States should also make it easier for nuclear family members to acquire a common citizenship or citizenships, both through easing the preconditions (such as residence periods) that apply before naturalization in such cases and through allowing renunciation of a former*

*nationality held by a subset of the family, where that is the free choice of persons who will not thereby be rendered stateless.*

(5)  *States of initial nationality should also reduce financial exactions and other penalties (such as barriers to inheritance) imposed on people who change their nationality.*

The central argument for dual nationality derives from the sociological reality that many people in today's world have deep and treasured connections to more than one national society, connections that are often fundamental to their own identities. Recognizing that reality outweighs the legal advantages—the greater clarity about obligations and rights—that would accrue from a world where each person has only one nationality. *This recognition reinforces the traditional rule of international law that nationality should reflect a genuine link between the individual and the state of citizenship.*[21] Accordingly,

(1)  *States should not sell citizenship to persons without any effective connection beyond purchase of nonresidential property or the payment of a citizenship fee.* Nationalities of convenience should be discouraged and may in most cases be disregarded by other states.

(2)  *Nationality should not be perpetuated to distant generations after the family has lost all real contact with the state involved.* States should require some lifetime link by a parent with the country of nationality (such as a specified period of personal residence) before that parent may transmit citizenship *jure sanguinis,* and may, if they wish, condition the continuation of the citizenship of a child born abroad on some later period of actual residence, as long as the conditions are not overly onerous. Permitting privileged acquisition of citizenship by more distant descendants of nationals would not be inconsistent with this genuine link principle, provided that the descendants themselves establish a new and viable link, primarily by taking up residence in the country.

## Permit Dual Nationals to Renounce a Nationality

Dual nationality is not an unalloyed good. The possibility of competing claims (particularly if the two states are deeply adversarial) or the desire to assure that all members of a family enjoy exactly the same citizenship status may well prompt a dual national to wish to surrender one nationality. States should readily offer the option of renunciation or denationalization to persons who make such a choice after full deliberation and with awareness of the consequences. This may be provided, as an option, to persons at the time of taking up a new nationality through naturalization, but it should also be available to others. One primary limitation should apply: Renunciation should not be allowed if it would render the person stateless, and it may be discouraged with respect to a country of nationality where the person intends to continue his or her residence.[22] The country whose citizenship is surrendered should also readily honor such a choice, although some carefully framed additional limits may sometimes be appropriate, such as, in connection with completion of military obligations or criminal sentences.

### Where Laws, Obligations, or Entitlements Conflict, Give Primacy to Principal Residence Country

In the private-law realm, conflict of law issues once resolved by reference to the law of the country of nationality should come increasingly to be governed by the law of the country of principal or habitual residence. (When the dual national resides in a country of which he or she is not a national, primacy should be given to the law of the country of nationality with which he or she has primary contacts.) Similarly, military obligations should run primarily to the country of principal residence; discharge of the obligation there (even when it involves no required service because that state does not conscript) should be held to discharge the obligation to other countries of nationality. Obviously this result can best be achieved through treaty. Several multilateral instruments embodying essentially this principle, including the 1997 European Convention and the 1930 Hague Protocol, already exist.

We recognize that requiring the identification of the country of principal residence or the country with which a person has primary contacts obviously substitutes a more vague standard for the clarity formerly provided by mono-nationality. This is admittedly a disadvantage, but multilateral treaties could help define more precise criteria for applying these tests.

As a corollary to this locus of primary duties, the dual national should look first to the country of principal residence for rights and entitlements. For example, that country's public assistance and social security systems should be the primary, and often the exclusive, source for that sort of aid, without prejudice to vested or accumulated rights in other contributory systems. The country of principal residence should also take the lead, where needed, in affording diplomatic protection. The rule permitting protection by the state of dominant and effective nationality, even as against other states of the person's nationality, should displace the old rule that disallowed diplomatic action in such circumstances.

*Surrender of Other Nationality for Those in Policy-Level
Positions in National Government*

In recent years, some dual nationals have served with distinction in such positions, particularly in situations where exiles have returned to participate in building democracy in states emerging from oppression. (Fortunately, the world has witnessed this type of governmental progression with some frequency over the last decade and a half.) Because of increasing convergence of interests and objectives among many states, dual nationals are not necessarily saddled with irreconcilable conflicts of interest in these circumstances. Nonetheless, many dual nationals have made a point of renouncing their distant allegiances before assuming high government office, even when returning from exile to a newly democratic state.

We recommend against such assumption of high-level policy and security-sensitive responsibilities by dual nationals, because interests and policies can change rather quickly. Suspicions directed against both the official and the other country of nationality can multiply quickly if policies implemented by a dual national, in the best of good faith, turn out badly. They can even spark serious incidents of hostility and mistrust, with lingering effects that will be hard to dispel. The risk that a bad outcome will be blamed on the other country of nationality is sufficiently great that both states may validly prescribe rules preventing such service by dual nationals. The state where the position exists may of course do so by imposing mono-nationality as a prerequisite to qualify for high-level service. But the choice is not solely for that country; the other country of nationality retains a significant interest to avoid any attribution of responsibility for the policies chosen by its citizen in making decisions for the first country. The second country may therefore also impose a rule against such service and implement it, if necessary, through enforced loss of nationality.

Dual nationals, however, should be permitted access to ordinary civil-service positions. We recognize that the dividing line between policy-level and other positions may sometimes be a difficult one to draw, but cabinet and immediate subcabinet positions in the national government may validly be reserved for mono-nationals, as may certain lesser positions involving highly sensitive national security functions.

# CHAPTER THREE

# Citizenship Policies
# and Political Integration

SINCE THE TIME OF ANCIENT ATHENS, citizenship has been closely linked
to political participation. In modern democratic states, many rights previously
enjoyed only by citizens have been disconnected from nationality and are now
granted to noncitizens on the basis of legal residence and employment or as
universal human rights. But nationality remains an important dividing line when
it comes to political participation. For immigrants, acquiring the nationality of
the host society has therefore always been the most important step toward political integration. We believe that it is important that immigrants can choose to
become citizens of their state of permanent residence and should also be encouraged to do so. Although we emphasize the priority of facilitating access to
formal citizenship, we suggest that it should be complemented by steps before
and after this threshold. Formal citizenship is not a sufficient condition for
political integration, nor need it be a necessary condition for enjoying certain
political rights.

Effective citizenship depends on structural opportunities for participation
and a widespread disposition to use them. Groups of immigrant origin are frequently underrepresented in the political process even when most of their members are nationals. We recommend various policies to prevent political
marginalization of such groups.

As we detail below, the easy assumption that political rights are congruent
with citizenship is not an accurate depiction of our world. Both human rights
law and domestic law affirm political rights for noncitizens, and the domestic

law of a number of states grants noncitizens voting rights. Promoting political participation for settled immigrants recognizes that they are, in the main, fully functioning members of the social and economic life of a society—they work, pay taxes, send their children to school, and attend places of worship. They have an interest in their communities and frequently have perspectives on local issues that enhance the consideration of public policies. They may also be victims of discrimination. All these factors argue in favor of political participation of noncitizens. Moreover, such participation is important training for the kind of engaged citizenship that most liberal democracies seek to foster. It can familiarize noncitizens with the political culture and imbue them with a sense of belonging that can make the decision to naturalize more attractive. Based on these considerations, we recommend ending restrictions of political liberties of noncitizen residents and granting them a local franchise.

### Political Participation Before Citizenship

*Political Liberties for Noncitizens*

Democracies are liberal if they guarantee all their citizens' basic liberties such as freedom of opinion, expression, peaceful assembly, and association. These liberties also apply to political activities, including those that involve criticism of, and opposition to, the government in power. Citizens participate in political life not only by casting their votes but also by debating politics in private and public arenas, by joining political parties or forming new ones, and by demonstrating in the streets. Today these liberties are no longer rights of citizens only; they have become universal human rights. Everyone regardless of nationality should enjoy them (United Nations 1948).

Many democratic states have in the past prohibited all political activities of noncitizens. A number of countries still have special constraints on the liberties of expression, assembly, and association for noncitizens.[23] Frequently, the national constitution empowers the legislature to enact such restrictions, even if parliaments do not always make use of this power. Some states deny foreign nationals the right to be members of political parties.[24] International law on human rights permits restrictions only if they "are necessary in a democratic society in the interests of national security or public safety, public order (*ordre public*), the protection of public health or morals, or the protection of the rights and freedoms of others" (ICCPR 1966: art. 22–23). We believe that policies denying immigrants' political liberties merely because of their foreign nationality are not sustainable.

It is occasionally suggested that allowing noncitizens to participate in political activities will lead to importing violent ethnic conflicts from their home countries. It is not plausible, however, that this danger can be avoided by making distinctions according to nationality. Naturalized citizens may engage in the same kind of activity while enjoying all liberties and a guaranteed right of residence. Prohibiting all political activities linked to such conflicts will also normally only serve to drive them underground. Laws that ban terrorist organizations, violent protest, or public speech that incites to violence are sufficient to deal with this threat and should generally be applied independently of the nationality of the persons who engage in such activities.

The right of immigrants to be members of, or to form, political parties deserves special consideration. It might be argued that because parties compete in elections, party membership ought to be limited to those who are enfranchised. However, parties also have the task of organizing and giving political expression to the various interests in society before and between elections. Groups of immigrant origin share important interests that need to be represented and translated into policy options. Immigrants should be encouraged to engage in this process, and party membership is one important way of doing this. In democratic states, parties are also essentially voluntary associations rather than institutions of government. While, as we will argue below, membership in national parliaments and candidacy in national elections may be restricted to citizens, the arguments used to support such policies do not carry through to mere party membership; being a member or even a functionary of a political party is not a public office. Finally, although noncitizens should have every right to form their own political associations outside the existing party system, forcing them to do so is bad policy. It enhances their segregation from the native population and makes it more likely that these associations will be dominated by "homeland" politics.

Even where the political liberties of noncitizens are not formally restricted, they may be curtailed in practice by wide-ranging and discretionary powers of deportation. States have legitimate interests in removing persons who pose imminent threats to national security or public safety. But to permit deportations for the exercise of political liberties has an obvious chilling effect on political participation. Accordingly, in the absence of a clear and present danger for national security, only those political activities that are punishable under criminal law should lead to deportations.

On the positive side, institutions of receiving states can encourage and promote forms of political activity that are conducive to integration. By forming their own associations and making their voices heard in political debates, immigrants become familiar with the political culture of the country and insert themselves into its political institutions. The freedom to engage in political activities has several integrative effects:

(1)   It permits immigrants to organize themselves, to articulate their interests, and to set their demands on the political agenda.

(2)   It helps to avoid or counterbalance paternalistic representation by organizations that promote the interests of immigrants but are run exclusively by native citizens.

(3)   It allows for a free articulation of differences of ideology, interests, and identities among migrants and undermines the perception that they are a homogeneous group of outsiders.

(4)   The experience and practice of democratic freedoms may also have an educational effect for those immigrants who come from less democratic countries. It shapes their outlook toward their country of origin and often turns emigrants into a force supporting democratic reform there.

### Franchise for Noncitizens: State Practice

While contemporary democratic states have generally granted resident foreigners political liberties, most do not allow them to vote or to be elected.[25] Many states do, however, permit their citizens living permanently abroad to participate in national elections. This raises the question why the franchise should be based on nationality rather than on residence.

Although voting rights for noncitizens are rather uncommon, there are several significant examples for such arrangements. In New Zealand, all permanent legal residents have enjoyed the general suffrage in all elections since 1975 (although not the right to be elected). In Great Britain, citizens from Commonwealth countries and Ireland not only can vote but also can run as candidates in elections at all levels. Ireland responded in 1985 by granting the national franchise to British citizens. It has also had local suffrage rights for all foreign residents since 1963 and eligibility for office since 1974. In 1975 Sweden introduced the vote for all noncitizens after three years of legal residence in local and regional elections and in referenda. Denmark, Finland, and Norway have similarly extended local voting rights that were originally granted only to citizens of Nordic countries. In 1985, the Netherlands adopted a local franchise independent of nationality after five years of residence. Thus, a franchise for noncitizens is not a utopian goal; it has become a democratic norm in several countries. There is no evidence that it undermines the integrity of the democratic process, and none of the countries that have introduced it since World War II has seriously considered abolishing it.

Variations in state practices regarding the franchise for noncitizens are generally linked to broader immigration and citizenship policies. (For an overview of franchise for noncitizens in selected countries, see table 4.) Some traditional immigration countries such as Australia, Canada, and the United States have not pursued noncitizen voting in part because they encourage immigrants to naturalize. Others states, such as Ireland, New Zealand, or the United Kingdom, tend to put less emphasis on naturalization and do not regard the franchise as being necessarily tied to formal citizenship. In contrast, Sweden and the Netherlands have extended the local franchise to all permanent residents in a deliberate effort to achieve political integration of their immigrant populations. In countries such as Germany or France, many debates and initiatives for a similar reform have not led to tangible results. Finally, Central and Eastern European countries that have only recently experienced substantial immigration have not even begun to seriously consider such a move.

Whatever these state-to-state differences, in most countries, rates of naturalization are lower than those of immigration. This makes democratic systems ever less representative of their populations, and thus the question of the franchise grows increasingly important.

As we spell out below, we believe granting noncitizens a franchise at the national level is not imperative if access to citizenship is sufficiently open. We do, however, make a general recommendation for a local franchise for immigrants who have been legal residents for several years.

*Arguments For and Against a National Franchise for Noncitizens*

Any discussion of the franchise for immigrants must consider the basic democratic premise that what concerns all should be decided by all. More specifically, persons who are subject to the laws of the state, who are currently informed about the issues at stake, and who will be affected by future legislation should not be excluded from electing representatives or running as candidates. Together, these considerations disqualify short-term visitors but not long-term residents. Most laws of democratic states apply not only to their citizens, but to all who live in the territory. Noncitizen immigrants pay taxes, but if they are disenfranchised they have no say over how the money is spent. Voters should also be well informed about candidates and issues on the political agenda. Permanent residents generally have just as much exposure to mass media and party campaigns as citizens have. Finally, most permanent residents will also have to bear the future consequences of political decisions in which they participate and are therefore likely to vote responsibly.

This is not yet a fully conclusive argument. If receiving countries adopt the proposals of chapter one of this report for facilitating access to citizenship, all long-term residents will have a chance to naturalize and most of their children will grow up as citizens. There are thus two routes toward equal political rights for immigrants and the native population: (1) extend the franchise; or (2) facilitate and promote access to citizenship. The question then becomes: Should foreign nationals be represented in political decisions even if they do not formally choose to become members of the political community? In states where naturalization is encouraged and offered on fair terms and where second and third generations are included through *jus soli* rules, the case for a noncitizen franchise loses much of its urgency. We believe that facilitating access to citizenship and granting noncitizen immigrants secure residence, full liberties, and welfare benefits are equally important tasks; if they are met, an extension of the general franchise is not an essential requirement.[26]

A general franchise for noncitizens, then, should not be seen as an imperative but rather as a legitimate political option. Different constitutional traditions and historic conceptions of citizenship may justify, as well as explain, policy differences in this area. For example, it may be difficult to reintroduce a franchise for noncitizens in the United States, which repudiated a fairly widespread practice of noncitizen voting around the turn of the twentieth century. As part of the process of European integration, however, member states of the European Union have accepted voting rights for nationals of the other member states.

The conclusion that states may legitimately choose to extend voting rights to noncitizens must still be defended against arguments that an immigrant franchise is detrimental to democracy or unfair toward citizens. Opponents of an immigrant franchise raise a number of other objections that refer to potential abuse, conflicts of loyalty, or lack of corresponding obligations. The first concern is that newcomers, who are unfamiliar with the political system and democratic norms, can be easily mobilized to cast their votes collectively and without proper consideration. This argument does not hold if a sufficient time of residence is required before the franchise can be exercised. The second objection is that foreign nationals may use their vote to promote the interests of their state of origin or to import its political conflicts. However, this applies just as well to dual nationals and even to those who have renounced their previous nationality. In some Western democracies, these concerns had served as pretexts for restricting political rights for naturalized citizens. With few remaining exceptions, such second-class citizenship for naturalized immigrants is today considered unacceptable. As with the general political liberties, the exercise of the franchise is also more likely to shape a democratic outlook than to be used for antidemocratic purposes. The third objection is raised in those countries where foreign nationals are exempted from citizenship obligations such as military or jury service. While conscription has indeed been an important historic element of citizenship, this is no longer the case today. The general duty to

Table 4.  *Overview of Franchise for Noncitizens in Project Countries*

| *Extent of Noncitizen Franchise* | Countries | | | | |
|---|---|---|---|---|---|
| Foreign residents in general elections | **New Zealand** Voting rights for all permanent residents since 1975 | | | | |
| Foreign residents in national referenda, regional and local elections | **Sweden** Franchise for all foreign residents after 3 years since 1975 | | | | |
| Foreign residents in local elections only | **Ireland** Local franchise for all foreign residents after 6 months since 1963 (since 1985 no residence requirements), for British citizens on national level since 1985 | **Netherlands** Franchise for all foreign residents after 5 years since 1985 | **Denmark** Franchise for all foreign residents after 3 years since 1981 (for Nordic citizens since 1977) | **Norway** Franchise for all foreign residents after 3 years since 1985 (for Nordic citizens since 1978) | **Finland** Franchise for all foreign residents after 4 years since 1991 (for Nordic citizens since 1981) |
| Postcolonial immigrants in all elections | **United Kingdom** Franchise for Commonwealth and Irish citizens at all levels since 1949 (now also for Scottish and Welsh assemblies) | | | | |
| Foreign residents in local or regional elections in some provinces only | **Switzerland** Canton Jura: voting rights at local and regional level for all foreign residents after 10 years since 1979, Canton Neuchâtel: voting rights at local level for all foreign residents after 5 years since 1849 | | | | |

| | **Spain** | **Portugal** | **Iceland** | **Israel** |
|---|---|---|---|---|
| Local franchise based on cultural similarity or reciprocity | Voting rights at local level under condition of reciprocity since 1985, eligibility at the local level under condition of reciprocity since 1992 | Franchise at local level under condition of reciprocity after 3 years since 1997 (previously restricted to nationals of Lusophone countries); citizens from Brazil and Cape Verde may vote (after 2 years) and stand as candidates (after 5 years) in national elections | Franchise at local level for citizens of Nordic Union since 1986 | Franchise at local level for immigrants under the Law of Return who refuse to acquire Israeli nationality since 1950 |
| Franchise based on supranational federation | **European Union Member States**<br>Franchise for EU citizens in other member states in local and European Parliament elections since 1992 | | | |
| No franchise for noncitizens | **United States**<br>Possibility of establishing local/state franchise where state constitutions and electoral law do not prohibit alien franchise (for example, Maryland) | **Australia**<br>Possibility of establishing local franchise in several provinces, where landed property is prerequisite | **Canada, Mexico, Japan**<br>No franchise for foreign nationals | |

*Note:* The term *voting rights* refers to the right to vote only; *franchise* includes the right to vote and eligibility, that is, the right to run as a candidate.

obey the laws and the duty to pay taxes is the same for citizens and noncitizens. Other legal obligations such as military conscription or jury service are not imposed on all citizens but on specific groups only or allow for numerous exemptions. If many citizens can vote while being exempted from these obligations, the argument from inequality of duties provides only weak support for rules that exclude noncitizens from the franchise. We believe therefore that these three objections are not persuasive.

### Restricted and Partial Franchise for Noncitizens

There are cases where the franchise is granted only to certain foreign nationals but not to others. The three major reasons for such special privileges are cultural affinity, reciprocity of rights, and supranational political integration. For example, in Portugal, Brazilian and Cape Verdean nationals enjoy a general franchise at the national level, whereas those from Scandinavian countries have a local right to vote based on reciprocity. The major example of a supranational regime is the EU where nationals of member states enjoy a local franchise and voting rights for the European Parliament when they reside in another state of the union. In all these cases we do not want to challenge the special grounds for extending the franchise to nationals of other countries, but we do question the reasons for excluding other immigrants from these arrangements.[27] From a democratic perspective, the relevant context for exercising the franchise is the domestic one of the society where an election takes place, not bilateral relations with other states. While the rights of foreign nationals ought to increase with their time of residence, they should not depend on their particular national origins. Global migratory flows are becoming increasingly diversified, and no immigration country can count on admitting only nationals of certain states with whom it entertains privileged relations. Rules of reciprocity would then create ever more different classes of foreign nationals. Special arrangements can nevertheless be useful as a first step. They break with the dogma that the franchise must be strictly tied to national citizenship, and they establish a level of rights that serves as a benchmark for the claims of third-country nationals. On the other hand, in a context of diverse immigration, their discriminatory character becomes more obvious. Why should an EU citizen who has just recently moved to another member state enjoy a right to vote in a local election while a third-country national who has lived there for years but does not yet qualify for naturalization is excluded from participating in his or her city?

Another restriction of the franchise, which is sometimes advocated and practiced in a few cases, is to grant foreign nationals voting rights but not eligibility to seek public office. This appears to conflict with a general democratic principle that voters can only be represented by other voters like themselves, not by a special class of persons who monopolize the right to hold public offices. But if naturalization is available and swift, then immigrants are not barred from running as candidates; they are merely asked to take this extra step of applying for citizenship. We think that a country such as New Zealand that grants national voting rights to noncitizens may reasonably argue that becoming a legislator requires a stronger and more lasting commitment than casting a vote. However, the case for this distinction is much less plausible at local and regional levels. In the Swiss cantons Neuchâtel and Jura, foreign residents participate in local elections (in Jura also in cantonal ones) but cannot run as candidates.[28] As we argue in the next section, nationality should not be seen as a relevant criterion for democratic representation in a local political community.

In a number of countries, noncitizens are not only denied access to elective public offices but are more broadly excluded from the civil service. We believe that political integration in a broader sense depends on an adequate representation of immigrants in all branches of public administration. Citizenship requirements are legitimate only in core areas that touch on sovereignty and security concerns (for example, professional positions in the army and diplomatic service). In some countries, however, civil service positions that are reserved for citizens cover a large sector of the labor market and include jobs for teachers in public schools, social workers, or even municipal workers such as street cleaners. This is unjustifiable discrimination and also bad policy from an integration perspective.

### Local Franchise for Noncitizens

Since the mid-1970s there has been a weak historical trend in Western Europe in favor of granting noncitizens a local or regional franchise, but not the national one. This is illustrated by the cases we have already mentioned (the Scandinavian states, the Netherlands, and EU citizenship). The Italian and French governments introduced such legislation in parliament in 1998 and 2000, respectively, but in both cases it was blocked because of constitutional objections or opposition in the second chamber. In most other countries of Western Europe, there have been similar political initiatives that have either failed to get sufficient support or have been struck down by constitutional courts. The Council of Europe has adopted a 1992 Convention on the Participation of Foreigners in Public Life at Local Level, which came into force in May 1997. Article 6(1) provides for the suffrage and eligibility for office for all foreign residents after five years.[29]

We believe that this hesitant trend should be more widely supported. The case for a noncitizen franchise is more powerful at local and regional levels than at the national one. Immigrants have specific interests in local politics and develop local identities. Most contemporary migrants are attracted to big cities and the economic and cultural opportunities they offer. In receiving countries, immigrants tend to develop an urban identity that can be easily combined with an ongoing national affiliation to their countries of origin. Even those who are not ready to join the wider political community of their host country feel that they have a stake in the city. This sense of belonging to the city can be expressed by participating in local elections. As members of low-income groups, immigrants are also particularly affected by policies in areas such as public housing, health services, and education where municipal authorities tend to have strong competencies. Granting them the franchise at the local level may thus provide political representation in decisions that affect their most immediate interests.

Second, some reasons for excluding noncitizens from the national elections do not apply at the local level. In contrast with a national polity, local political communities have no immigration control that distinguishes between citizens and noncitizens. The right of free movement within the territory of a democratic state is not tied to nationality (United Nations 1948; ICCPR 1966).[30] Membership in a municipality or federal province shifts automatically with a change of residence. Furthermore, the argument that foreign nationals are exempted from some obligations of citizenship does not apply at the municipal level. In the main, local citizenship has no specific legal duties that are exclusively imposed on citizens.[31]

With minor modifications these arguments apply also to regional or provincial elections. Settled immigrants enjoy the same right to interregional mobility as citizens, but they are less likely to see the regional level as essential to their interests and identities. In federal states, where regions enjoy substantial autonomy, provincial elections are more likely to be regarded as similar to national ones, whereas in unitary states they are more like local ones, where regional authorities have primarily administrative tasks. Such differentiations apply also to the franchise in citizen petitions, referenda, and plebiscites. When the outcome is consultative rather than binding for the legislature and when the question asked does not concern constitutional matters, then there is little reason to deny resident noncitizens a right to cast their vote.[32] We suggest therefore that noncitizen residents should be able to participate in these consultative plebiscites at the national level even in countries where they have no franchise in parliamentary elections.

Some people object to extending the local franchise on grounds that this will divert attention and political pressure from the more important task of reforming nationality laws. We agree that the latter ought to be given priority. The local franchise is no substitute for access to full citizenship. However, these two routes to political integration are also not opposed to each other. In Sweden and the Netherlands, both reforms were part of a broader package. Moreover, easier naturalization does not make a local franchise redundant. As we have argued, there are good reasons for extending the vote to immigrants who have become full members of a municipality but do not want to adopt the nationality of their host country.

An argument may be lodged against the local franchise on formal grounds, based on the premise that in a democracy "the people" are a single and indivisible collective and that the right to vote belongs only to members of that collective. Because provinces and municipalities are merely political subdivisions of the larger polity, their electorate represents a regional section of the sovereign people and therefore can only include persons eligible to participate in national elections.[33] We do not share this view. We have argued that admission of new members is different at national and local levels; naturalization involves a declaration of intent, but local citizenship follows automatically from residence in the municipality. Even those who would not like to grant the national franchise to immigrants before they have signed a "naturalization compact" should therefore accept that such a requirement is arbitrary for local voting rights. In the EU, the unitary conception of the democratic people, which is still used as an argument against the local franchise for third-country nationals, has already been officially abandoned. By ratifying the Treaty of Maastricht, all member states have accepted that in their countries the local electorate includes foreign nationals who are not enfranchised in national elections.

General conditions for exercising the local franchise (such as age thresholds or a certain period of residence in the municipality) should be the same for national and foreign citizens. It is, however, a reasonable demand that noncitizens live in the country for a period of years before enjoying voting rights.[34] As we have argued above, a democratic franchise assumes that those who vote have lived under the laws for some time and have had a chance to become familiar with parties, candidates, and political issues to be decided. For the local franchise, such a general residence requirement must not exceed the general waiting period for naturalization. Indeed, we recommend a somewhat shorter length of time, which would underline that the local franchise is not regarded as an alternative to naturalization, but as one step in an ongoing process of political integration.[35] Participating in local elections can then be seen as training for full citizenship, which is acquired through naturalization. In countries where permanent residence permits can be acquired only after renewal of initial temporary ones, the local franchise should be tied to permanent residence.[36] This would highlight the symbolic importance of this status. The receiving society signals in this way that it has accepted an immigrant as a prospective citizen with the right to participate in its political life. A secure status of permanent residence is also important for encouraging noncitizen voters to participate. Immigrants whose residence or employment permits are limited and can be easily revoked will be less inclined to engage in political life. Such legal insecurity focuses their interests on more immediate economic targets and reinforces an orientation to return to their countries of origin.

Democratic elections are not only held to choose persons or assemblies that exercise legislative or executive power within a certain territory. The composition of bodies representing sectoral interests—such as local and regional school boards, works councils, chambers of labor and commerce, or student parliaments—is usually determined by democratic vote as well. One can find a few instances of legislation that bars foreign nationals from voting or running as candidates in such elections.[37] We believe that such discrimination is arbitrary and should be abolished. Nationality is manifestly irrelevant for the purposes of these organizations as well as for determining membership in their electorate. Such organizations do not participate in the exercise of sovereign political power, and their constituencies are defined by shared interests or institutional affiliations.

In some European countries there is a strong tradition of organized cooperation between government institutions and organizations representing sectoral interests. Where this is the case, public policy should not only be concerned with removing barriers of eligibility but should encourage these organizations to actively recruit immigrants and persons of immigrant origin for their governing boards. This will make such bodies more representative and responsive to the needs of their constituency and will directly contribute to the overall political integration of lawfully settled immigrants.

### Promoting Political Participation Among Groups of Immigrant Origin

Communities of immigrant origin include citizens as well as noncitizen residents. The political integration of these ethnic minorities depends not only on their individual rights (which are formally equal for those among their members who are citizens) but also on opportunities and incentives for their participation in political life. Access to political rights through admission to citizenship or through extending the franchise to noncitizens is not enough if such minorities have lower voting rates in elections and are strongly underrepresented in public offices, parliaments, and political parties. What can be done to promote the political participation of groups of immigrant background?

Although most democratic states do not oblige their citizens to vote, there is certainly a public interest in facilitating and encouraging political participation as a form of active citizenship.[38] High rates of participation strengthen the democratic legitimacy of political authority and may also promote political community through a shared sense of common responsibilities. Low participation rates correlate strongly with socioeconomic status and thus create a class bias in democratic politics. The political participation of ethnic and racial minorities should be a special concern. In democratic societies, minority groups are more vulnerable when they are politically isolated. They are more easily targeted as outsiders, cannot voice their own interests, and often come to be regarded as second-class citizens. To be sure, some minorities may want to insulate themselves and refrain from participation in political life. For most groups of immigrant origin, however, low rates of political participation do not result from their own choices but are due to various circumstances, some of which can be influenced by public policy.

It is neither necessary nor reasonable to expect communities of immigrant origin to participate or to be elected in proportion to their numbers of the population, given the distinctive characteristics and priorities of immigrants settling in a new country. Where these groups have high percentages of recent arrivals, or of people who plan to return to their country of origin, or of people who come from countries with no tradition of democratic participation, it is highly likely that they will have lower rates of participation, even where the host society enables and encourages their participation.[39] So lower rates of participation are not, by themselves, evidence of any unfairness in the institutions of the host society. Indeed, it could be argued that a goal of proportional representation for groups of immigrant origin would run counter to integrative ideals—that is, an important indicator of successful political integration might be when persons from a minority background are considered as candidates for public office as individuals and not as representatives of their group.

While these considerations have force, we may nonetheless be concerned about conditions of persistent underrepresentation of immigrant-origin communities. Such underrepresention may indicate structural barriers to participation and social marginalization of ethnic minorities, particularly where it exists for long-settled populations. The goal, therefore, should not be to guarantee proportional representation of groups of immigrant origin, but rather to identify and remove structural and social barriers to effective participation.

## Legislative and Administrative Obstacles to Participation

Where citizenship is a precondition for the franchise, restrictive naturalization policies may pose a significant obstacle to immigrant participation and representation in politics. This provides an additional reason to those presented in chapter one for naturalization rules and procedures that are reasonable, transparent, and nondiscretionary. Democratic states should also conduct periodic naturalization campaigns. State-sponsored naturalization activities send a signal to political parties that they have to compete for newly enfranchised voters, and they enhance the awareness of the native population that immigrant-origin communities have a right to participate in political decisions.

It is well established that voting procedures have an impact on participation levels. Complex registration rules and difficult-to-follow voting instructions are likely to pose special problems for immigrant communities. States ought to ensure that official documents and announcements relating to elections be issued in the languages of major immigrant groups. Bilingual ballots have become a hotly contested issue in some states of the United States. We believe they are important for two independent reasons: first, because voters should be as fully informed as possible; and second, because bilingual ballots have a strong symbolic message—they demonstrate not only an appreciation of minority cultures but also an effort to foster immigrant participation.

Multilingual information and ballots have to be combined with efforts to improve the knowledge of the dominant language among immigrant voters. It is not sufficient for minorities just to receive relevant information about elections in their native tongue; they should also be able to form and reconsider their political preferences in debates with citizens of different ethnic backgrounds. To enhance democratic deliberation, then, states need to provide instruction in national languages and strong incentives for newcomers to enroll.

Voting systems may raise an additional barrier to effective participation and representation of communities of immigrant origin. In majoritarian systems in particular, electoral districting can dilute representation either by dividing compact areas of minority settlement or by packing immigrant communities into districts in which they represent supermajorities. In proportional representation systems, ethnic minority parties are sometimes locked out of any seats in parliament by threshold requirements. Native racial and linguistic minorities have sometimes benefited from affirmative policies or special exemptions. For example, in Germany, the 5 percent threshold for party representation in parliament does not apply to delegates of the Danish minority in the province of Schleswig-Holstein; and Poland, Hungary, and Romania have similar exemptions for national minority representation. We do not recommend such arrangements for groups of recent immigrant origin. As we have argued above, proportional representation is not a reasonable target for such groups. Instead, rules concerning the aggregation of votes should be scrutinized for adverse effects on these groups that diminish their chances of fair representation on equal terms with the general population.

### Enabling Political Participation

The second area of relevant public policies concerns background conditions that have an impact on political participation rates. Policies that improve the social and cultural integration of groups of immigrant origin will also have positive effects on their political integration. Empirical research shows that low levels of education, unskilled jobs, poor housing, and high percentages of single-person households are major factors that contribute to lower political participation. Not all of these factors can be easily influenced by public policies. However, family reunification and public welfare benefits are two policy areas where governments shape the conditions for political integration. (We pursue a detailed discussion of the latter kinds of policies in chapter four.)

Political participation depends not only on the socioeconomic position of individuals within the group but also on the internal structure of minority communities and their interaction with the native population. Participation in civil society prepares immigrants for political participation and provides them with influence in the policy-making process. Integration into civil society is not a one-way street of assimilation into the institutions of mainstream society but also offers opportunities for groups of immigrant origins to organize around their specific interests and identities as ethnic minorities. Both forms of participation will generally contribute to political integration. Empirical research confirms that rates of voting rise significantly with the membership of groups of immigrant origin in associations of mainstream society such as churches, sports and leisure clubs, trade unions, or neighborhood committees. However, even a tendency of certain groups to "stick to themselves" by forming their own ethnic associations may have positive effects (depending to some extent on the political orientation of leaderships). Where such associations communicate across religious and political cleavages or form larger umbrella organizations, they are more likely to encourage their members to participate in the political life of their society of residence.

The lesson for public policy is that municipal and national administrations should support the formation of associational networks and consult them regularly on immigration and integration policies as well as on general issues affecting all citizens.[40] Formal or informal consultation mechanisms can be important instruments for political integration, creating relations of trust between public administrations and spokespersons of communities of immigrant origin. They also serve as two-way transmission belts for integration policies:

Minorities can voice grievances and suggest policy reforms in a low-confrontation setting; public administrators can obtain information and foster cooperation in the implementation of their programs.

Many European cities have established consultative bodies on immigrant policies. The members of these committees are appointed by municipal authorities, designated by ethnic minority associations, or elected by the ethnic minority communities themselves. Even though democratic elections for consultative committees obviously strengthen the mandate of representatives, they should not be accepted as a surrogate for the local franchise. Such consultative bodies are special arrangements for making a public administration more responsive toward a particular group, whereas a local franchise for noncitizens establishes a common local citizenship shared by all residents.

Apart from encouraging the collective self-organization and participation of groups of immigrant origins in political life, there is also a need for citizenship education programs that provide the individual members of these groups with the necessary knowledge and motivation for participating effectively in the political process. Language training and courses in civics should be offered on a wide basis especially for newcomers and applicants for naturalization. Certificates of courses taken by newcomers should count toward corresponding naturalization requirements. Such courses may be offered by a variety of institutions such as local public administration, employers, organizations of adult education, or nongovernmental organizations working with immigrants. Private institutions should have to meet quality standards but should also be subsidized for providing this important service. To participate effectively, immigrants must become familiar with the dominant language and the political institutions of the receiving society; at the same time, native citizens must also be educated about the changes and challenges brought about by immigration. This is an important task for public schools, mass media, and neighborhood initiatives. The goal of such educational programs is not just to spread information about the history, culture, and languages of immigrant groups and their countries of origin, but to combat racist and xenophobic attitudes and behavior and to shape a common identity of citizenship that is more inclusive than the traditional national identities of the native population.

### Agenda for Democratic Parties

In modern democracies, parties are the most important political players. The political integration of groups of immigrant origin depends not only on removing discriminatory legislation and implementing public policy reforms but also on the attitudes of political parties.

Increasing the rates of representation of ethnic minorities in parliamentary assemblies and public offices largely depends on whether political parties are willing to endorse candidates of immigrant origin. Putting such candidates on party lists for winnable seats has also a strong positive effect on voter turnout in minority communities. Political parties are therefore crucial when it comes to reducing both representation and participation deficits.

Proportional representation systems make it easier for parties to put minority candidates on their lists in winnable positions even where they could not achieve an overall majority within the local constituency. In such systems, political parties should include ethnic origin as one among the many criteria they take into consideration when selecting candidates who will appeal to a broad range of their potential voters. In majoritarian voting systems, geographically dispersed minority groups will have fewer chances to achieve party nominations for candidates who represent their group.[41] However, as we have noted, candidates of immigrant origin should not be regarded as representing only their ethnic group. Winning seats in constituencies where few voters share their biographical background may mark important progress in political integration.

The willingness of a party to present such candidates will depend to some extent on its ideological orientation and strategic calculations. If groups of immigrant origin are overwhelmingly identified with one party, other parties may believe that it makes little sense to include them on their lists. We believe that this is a shortsighted view. These groups are not a homogeneous electorate. A party may attract their votes because it defends the general socioeconomic interests of lower income groups, because its program responds to specific political interests of groups of immigrant origin, or because its general ideological outlook appeals to the religious values of those communities. Often, different parties represent these various interests. Support from groups of immigrant origin is also important for all political parties because such groups generally contain a large share of first-time voters, who are likely to maintain their loyalty to the party for which they first vote.[42]

The chances that naturalized immigrants will be selected as candidates on a party ticket depend also on the internal structures of the party organization. Immigrant and ethnic minority caucuses within parties can be effective instruments for putting immigrant demands on a party platform and candidates of immigrant origins into winnable positions. There are different models for such internal party organizations. Some develop from rank and file initiatives, bringing together party stalwarts of the same ethnic origins who try to mobilize their constituency in election campaigns. Others are initiated by the party leadership and charged with providing policy expertise for legislative initiatives. We do not want to prescribe a specific way to organize groups of immigrant origins but merely emphasize the importance of organizational remedies for reducing a common representation deficit within democratic parties.

Finally, political parties are also responsible for creating and supporting a wider political culture where racism and xenophobia are kept at bay. In democratic states, electoral campaigns frequently create temptations for scapegoating minorities who are the target of widespread prejudice among the majority population. Minorities of immigrant origin are especially vulnerable in this regard if they include a large percentage of noncitizens who cannot defend themselves in the voting booth. In many Western immigration countries, parties and candidates have campaigned on stridently anti-immigrant platforms. Their opportunities to grow and achieve positions of power strongly depend on the other parties' attitudes. Unfortunately, many parties at the center of the ideological spectrum have not refrained from playing the race and immigration cards to prevent a swing of their electorate toward right-wing populists.

Democratic parties should create a broad cross-party consensus on two points. First, while democratic parties will obviously disagree on many issues of immigration and immigrant policy, they ought to avoid any stigmatization of groups of immigrant origin in their own propaganda and policy proposals. Second, democratic parties should refrain from forming government coalitions or any other political alliance with political parties that promote or incite racial and ethnic prejudice against groups of immigrant background.[43]

### Recommendations

A core idea informs our analyses and recommendations on political integration: Democratic countries that receive substantial immigration must reform their citizenship policies so that those migrants who settle in their territories do not remain shut out from its public political life. Such policies should combine access to the nationality of their host country with political rights and duties independent of nationality. Permitting and encouraging the political participation of long-term resident immigrants makes the democratic process more representative. This enhances its general legitimacy, improves the quality of decision making in matters that concern groups of immigrant origin, and makes these groups less vulnerable to xenophobia or racism in politics and in the wider society.

From this context, then, we derive specific guidelines for policy reform:

(1) *Basic liberties such as the freedom of thought, expression, association, and assembly are human rights that must not depend on nationality.* Noncitizens ought to be able to exercise these freedoms in their political activities within the same limits that apply to nationals.

(2) *Under the condition that states open admission to citizenship through naturalization and automatic acquisition, they may reserve core political rights, such as access to high public office or the right to vote in national elections, for their nationals.*

(3) *Local franchise should derive from legal permanent residence.* In contrast with general elections, nationality ought not to be a relevant criterion for democratic representation in a local political community.

(4) *Electoral systems should be scrutinized for overt and hidden barriers that diminish opportunities for members of groups of immigrant origin to vote, to run for office, or to be elected.* Equal rights are not enough to achieve effective political participation and equitable representation of these groups.

(5) *Public policies should encourage the participation of groups of immigrant origin in civil society.* Political authorities should establish mechanisms of cooperation and consultation that involve associations of these groups in processes of policy formation and implementation.

(6) *Democratic political parties should provide opportunities for candidates of immigrant origins to run as candidates on their lists.* They ought to refrain from stigmatizing ethnic minorities in their campaigns and from alliances with other parties that stir up ethnic prejudice and racial hatred.

# CHAPTER FOUR

# Social Rights
# and Citizenship

LIBERAL-DEMOCRATIC STATES generally offer citizens benefits and entitlements on an equal basis—what T. H. Marshall referred to in a famous essay as
"the basic human equality associated with full membership of a community"
(Marshall 1950: 8). In the current era of immigration, there are strong arguments for extending these entitlements beyond citizens to include settled, foreign nationals: especially those in *jus sanguinis* states where several generations may be noncitizens. These arguments are based on equity principles. Settled
foreign nationals pay taxes, obey the law, assume other social and community
obligations, and are subject to the vicissitudes of the market that affect citizens
and noncitizens alike. Arguments for equal treatment can also be based on the
fact that withholding benefits imposes social costs. Restrictions can create
spillover effects on the citizen members of immigrant families and expose other
members of society to the health and other hazards associated with excluding
residents from health care, education, and other basic social supports.

As a result, many, but not all, liberal states that have witnessed high historical levels of immigration at the end of the twentieth century have provided
settled foreign nationals with access to benefits and to labor markets more or
less on a par with citizens. In this chapter we address the question of whether or
not access to the social welfare state and to the labor market should be rationed
on the basis of citizenship in liberal democracies.

The use of citizenship rather than long-term residence to ration public benefits raises significant concerns. Restrictive policies, like those enacted by the

U.S. Congress in 1996, can increase hardship, impose disproportionate burdens on immigrant families and the citizen children who live within them, slow integration, send exclusionary signals, and give citizenship a meaning quite different from the civic engagement many hope it connotes.

National labor policies that restrict settled foreign nationals' access to private employment are relatively rare. Policies that deny permanent residents access to public employment and self-employment, however, are more common and are often overly broad in character. The immigration countries of Australia, Canada, and the United States offer legal immigrants strikingly open access to the labor market—access that accrues not just with citizenship or long-term residence, but from the date most immigrants receive a legal status. As a result, these immigration nations extend labor market rights to legal noncitizens that exceed even the most inclusionary proposals now being advanced within the EU. This open access, coupled with extensive antidiscrimination protections, appears to play an important role in the comparatively rapid economic integration of the second generation in United States.

In this chapter, we recommend that citizenship status not be the gatekeeper to access to social benefits and the labor market. Rather, foreign nationals who have a status that authorizes or presumes settlement in the state should be guaranteed eligibility on terms similar to those established for citizens. We adopt the term *presumptive permanent residence* to describe the status of noncitizens in this category. Adopting this broader understanding of membership, we suggest, complements and supports the institution of citizenship in liberal democracies.

### Rationale for the Inquiry

Liberal democracies have steadily moved from citizenship to personhood, or at least presumptive permanence, when allocating social rights. (By social rights we mean access to contributory and noncontributory social benefits, access to social investments such as job training, and access to the labor market.) This development represents a major postwar victory for liberalism (Joppke 1994; Soysal 1994). Why then explore the relationship of citizenship to social rights if the link between them is breaking down?

First, broader conceptions of membership are not necessarily secure. The shrinking of the welfare state in many industrialized countries and the periodic rise of anti-immigrant sentiment have led to policy proposals and new legislation that curb immigrants' access to benefits and work. This countertrend has been forcefully in evidence the United States, where in 1996 Congress enacted new policies that restricted legal permanent residents' access to many important public benefits until naturalization. These policies shifted the bright line that once defined membership in U.S. society from legal residence to citizenship, thereby reestablishing the importance of citizenship in allocating social rights.

Second, the policies we examine were enacted during a period of decline in Europe's working age population arising from low fertility rates and increased longevity. The policy changes also occur within the context of a more mobile flow of transnational residents: settlers who maintain lives in one or more nation-states and who may or may not be citizens of each. And they take place within the context of a forty-year shift in the source of migration flows from developed to developing countries.[44] These migration and population trends mean that flows to industrialized countries are increasingly composed of ethnic and racial minorities, many of whom enter with comparatively low education levels. The new entrants are coming to represent a larger and larger segment of the host country's labor force. Each of these characteristics—being a visible minority, noncitizen status, low education credentials, and centrality to the labor force—suggests the importance of policies that promote social rights and integration and calls into question policies that ration benefits on the basis of citizenship.

### Analytic Framework

States have adopted a range of general rules that define a set of noncitizens' social rights. These include access to:

- the labor market, including noncitizens' ability to freely choose a career, a workplace, or self-employment;
- noncontributory social welfare programs (defined as cash transfer, child assistance, housing assistance, health care, and health insurance programs);
- contributory social insurance programs (old age and pension programs as well as unemployment insurance); and
- selected social investment programs such as job training, grants and loans for higher education, integration assistance, and elementary and secondary education.

We have examined in detail policies regarding access to social benefits and the labor market in nine representative liberal industrialized democracies. Five are self-consciously nations of immigration: Australia, Canada, France, Israel, and the United States; and four are de facto immigration nations within the European Union: Austria, Germany, the Netherlands, and the United Kingdom. These countries reflect substantial variation in the size and character of immigration flows, as well as differing regimes of access to both the social welfare state and labor market, and approaches to the grant of citizenship.

The many different legal statuses assigned to residents can be grouped into four general categories and ranked hierarchically with regard to membership rights:

- *Citizens*—a category that includes some noncitizens who enter as virtual citizens (for example, ethnic Germans who are granted citizenship upon request);
- *EU citizens*—citizens in EU member countries granted full social rights across the union provided they are employed or self-employed;[45]
- *Presumptively permanent noncitizens*—long-settled noncitizens and other immigrants entitled by law to settled residence in the state (for example, recognized refugees, persons authorized upon admission to reside permanently, and persons who attain such a right after a period of residence in the state);[46]
- *Presumptively temporary noncitizens*—noncitizens whose presence is invited or tolerated for a limited period of time and whose return is anticipated. Members of this group must change their legal status if they wish to reside or work in the host country after the period of time for which they have been admitted ends (for example, students, guest workers, and asylum seekers).

We restrict our analysis to legal or tolerated immigrants, ignoring the undocumented or illegal immigrant population. For the most part, undocumented immigrants' lack of immigration status precludes their access to any public assistance.[47] The detailed results of our examination of benefits policies for legal immigrants are set out in appendix I.

### Access to Public Benefits: General Policy Trends

Most of the nations examined here make presumptively permanent residents eligible for the constellation of noncontributory and contributory benefits programs provided to citizens.[48] In some instances, recently arrived immigrants (citizens of an EU nation or "return" immigrants in Germany and Israel) are accorded full social and labor market rights upon entry. Their treatment is in sharp contrast to the third-country nationals who constitute a majority of EU immigrants and whose social and labor rights accrue over time. These third-country nationals from outside the EU typically need to establish permanent status or naturalize to obtain access to labor and welfare rights. Accordingly, rationing of benefits occurs by granting or withholding established immigrant status.

Immigrants whose presence is considered temporary and whose return is expected enjoy fewer rights, and their eligibility varies widely across nations. In fact, the immigrants who can be classified as temporary immigrants constitute a heterogeneous class. The group is composed of those who are in a probationary phase and on their way to established status as well as those who are in the process of eventual voluntary or involuntary return from the host nation.

*Path to Permanent Status*

It is important to recognize the degree to which each nation's *integration* policies are bound up in its *immigration* policies. Put simply, citizenship for many European nations is essentially a three-stage (or even more graduated) process that generally ascends from temporary to established status and then to citizenship.

In contrast, progress to citizenship in certain immigration countries— Australia, Canada, and the United States—generally occurs in two stages, with the immigrant entering as a legal permanent resident or landed immigrant and then converting to citizenship.[49] Accordingly, many of the comparisons we make are between this first stage in the immigration nations (that is, those of permanent resident or landed immigrant status) and Europe's second stage (established immigrant).[50]

Within most European countries, making the transition from temporary to permanent immigration status is a lengthy and often onerous task, especially for third-country nationals.[51] These third-country nationals often hold a temporary status for four to five years before being authorized to apply for a more permanent immigration status.[52] Receipt of permanent status is typically dependent upon proof that the petitioner:

- is employed and his or her employment conforms to established labor quotas;
- has sufficient income and/or housing for him or herself and family members;
- knows the native language; and
- is of good moral character (that is, has no criminal record).

While the conditions for making the transition from temporary to permanent status vary widely across nations of the EU, the share of third-country nationals with established status appears to be roughly similar. In Austria, 55 percent hold established permit status; in France, 66 percent. Fifty-five percent of Turkish nationals in Germany hold unrestricted residence permits (Groenendijk, Guild, and Barzilay 2001).

As noted in chapter one, the time period for the subsequent transition from permanent residence to citizenship varies across nations. In Australia, legal immigrants can naturalize two years after entry. Noncitizens in France, the Netherlands, the United Kingdom, and the United States are eligible for naturalization after five years of permanent residency status (spouses of U.S. citizens may naturalize in the United States in three years). Longer periods generally hold in Germany, where the wait is a minimum of eight years under the usually applicable rules, and in Austria, where noncitizens may wait anywhere from ten to thirty years before obtaining citizenship (Groenendijk, Guild, and Barzilay 2001). All the countries in our study, with the exception of Austria, have established *jus soli* principles for conferring citizenship on second- and third-generation immigrants, typically making citizenship immediately available to third-generation immigrants and widely available to second-generation immigrants once they reached the age of majority.

### *Rationing Benefits by Citizenship: The United States, Austria, and the United Kingdom*

As noted previously, presumptive permanent residence is usually accompanied by eligibility for social benefits made available to citizens. There are, however, important exceptions in some countries including the United States, Austria, and the United Kingdom. Under the welfare legislation passed by the U.S. Congress in 1996, permanent resident aliens are denied federal health insurance, nutrition benefits, welfare and related work supports, and aid to the aged and disabled. (Exceptions are made for immigrants who have worked for ten years in formal or "covered" employment, refugees and asylees, and noncitizens who have served in the military.) The $20 billion in savings over five years these restrictions were expected to generate would have accounted for half of the welfare reform law's total savings.

The United States has not been alone in rationing benefits in this manner. Roughly half of Austrian provinces bar third-country nationals (that is, foreign- and native-born residents who do not hold EU citizenship) from their social assistance programs altogether. And in other provinces third-country nationals receive lower benefits than citizens. Third-country nationals are also barred from receiving housing subsidies that would permit them to buy or build houses, and they are prohibited from renting any subsidized flats owned by the municipality of Vienna (Groenendijk, Guild, and Barzilay 2001).

In 1999, the United Kingdom enacted the Asylum and Immigration Act of 1999, a law that resembles the U.S. welfare law's immigrant restrictions. The law bars presumptively permanent third-country nationals (excluding refugees) from noncontributory social programs for five years following entry, at which point they would be entitled to apply for established status. This law is based on the premise that to qualify for "indefinite leave to remain" status in the United Kingdom (that is, presumptive permanent residence), third-country nationals must prove that they have sufficient income and housing and that they and any family members have had no recourse to public funds.[53]

### Indirect Bars to Benefits

In addition to these explicit bars, less direct restrictions are also evident. In Germany and Austria, for example, many permanent immigrants' de facto eligibility for social welfare benefits can be undermined by the state's authority to withdraw work or residence permits if the noncitizen becomes dependent on public aid. In practice, however, withdrawal of residence permits and expulsion are extremely rare for established immigrants in Germany.[54] A similar situation exists in the United States, where the federal government has rarely exercised its statutory authority to remove legal permanent residents who become dependent on public benefits within five years of admission.

Nations' restrictions on noncitizen benefit use can also take the form of new sponsorship requirements. For example, the English-speaking immigration countries (Australia, Canada, and the United States) introduced new controls in the mid-1990s that shift the legal obligations for immigrants' support from the state to their sponsors. The support requirement's duration varies across countries, as does its scope.[55] Immigrant families in the United States are expected to pay for health insurance; in Canada and Australia they are not. In each case, though, the obligation is lifted when the immigrant becomes a citizen, thereby creating a powerful incentive to naturalize. By creating these new incentives to naturalize, policy makers have altered immigrants' motive for seeking citizenship, giving instrumental concerns greater weight than before and subordinating, perhaps, motives of national loyalty and solidarity.[56]

### Restrictions to Contributory Benefit Programs

Although Austria, Germany, the United Kingdom, and the United States have restricted permanent residents' use of noncontributory public benefits, noncitizen use of contributory public benefits is less limited.[57] Eligibility for these contributory benefits is typically triggered by participation in the labor force. Because contributory public benefits are usually tied to employment, a country's labor and antidiscrimination legislation will have a powerful influence on the participation of presumptively permanent foreign nationals in contributory public programs such as unemployment insurance and pensions.

Some distinctions between established noncitizens and citizens have been drawn in the nations examined, however. Austria, for example, provides a lower benefit to presumptively permanent immigrants resident for less than eight years (Waldrauch 2000).

### Does Rationing Benefits by Citizenship Make Good Policy?

A number of arguments may be offered in support of limiting noncitizens' access to public benefits. First, income disparities between developed and developing countries are so wide that benefits offered by the host country can exceed income opportunities in the sending countries. As a result, nations that offer immigrants generous benefits may serve as a magnet for poor immigrants who would qualify for subsidies and may repel higher-earning immigrants who would contribute tax dollars to pay for the benefits. Thus, welfare's availability changes the composition of the immigration flow and enables some unintegrated immigrants to stay who would have otherwise returned.

Second, noncitizens are said to represent a disproportionately large share of welfare users, imposing high costs on taxpayers.[58] This drain on state resources may jeopardize the social contract that maintains the welfare state and turn public opinion against more inclusive immigration policies. It might also be argued that an immigrant's support should fall to his or her sponsor, who benefits from being able to unite with a family member or by obtaining a new employee (or both, in some instances).

Finally, it is suggested that restricting benefits to citizens provides an incentive to naturalize. The naturalization process, in turn, has an independent integrating effect produced by requirements to learn the language and to develop at least a rudimentary historical, political, and cultural understanding of the host country.[59]

At the same time, however, rationing benefits by citizenship raises substantial concerns. In the first instance, such schemes discriminate against presumptively permanent residents by putting them in the position of having to contribute to the state without receiving the reciprocal benefits that flow to other members.

Second, restrictions on rights may give citizenship an increasingly instrumental value as foreign nationals naturalize to obtain safety net or work support services or to relieve their sponsors of a binding support contract. The resulting conception of citizenship may be viewed as at odds with the nation-building goal of promoting durable and wholehearted civic engagement. (It should be noted, however, that the possession of citizenship—whatever the motivation for its acquisition—may result in deep sentiments of attachment and belonging over time.)

Third, restrictions on noncitizens' access to noncontributory benefits imposed by Austria, the United Kingdom, and the United States raise integration concerns. In the United States, the families who have been cut off from social benefits by new citizenship restrictions are among the neediest. Immigrant children in the United States are more likely to be poor, to live in overcrowded housing, and to report being in poor health than children of natives. Not surprisingly, they are far less likely to be insured or to have a usual source of care than their counterparts in families headed by a citizen (Capps 2001). Similar results, presumably, would obtain in the other industrialized countries that have introduced benefit restrictions. Restricted access to public health insurance, coupled with the diminished medical care that results, therefore, can lead to poor and declining health outcomes for children. It is also likely that limiting access to publicly subsidized work supports such as childcare, transportation assistance, and job and language training will slow immigrants' labor force mobility. Furthermore, policies that bar immigrants from cash transfers also generally bar them from these kinds of work supports. Denying noncitizens these basic work supports can only slow economic integration.

Fourth, restricting legal noncitizens' access to public benefits—especially in *jus soli* nations—has unintended and arguably discriminatory spillover effects on citizen children. In the United States three-quarters of all children in immigrant families (that is, with one or more foreign-born parents) are citizens (Fix and Zimmerman 1999). Since enactment of the welfare legislation in the United States in 1996, there has been a reduction in benefits use not just among the noncitizen adults who were the policies' targets, but also among the citizen children who live in their families and within the same, typically constrained, family budget.

Fifth, federal benefit restrictions decouple the national government's role as gatekeeper from its responsibility for paying the costs of newcomers' settlement. These costs, then, fall disproportionately on the receiving community. To the extent that state and local governments follow the national government's lead in erecting eligibility restrictions, noncitizens are likely to suffer more limited freedom of movement than their citizen counterparts. As the decision to grant or deny health and other benefits falls increasingly to subnational units of government, levels of food insecurity, and health care access and outcomes among noncitizens may vary more widely than among citizens.

Finally, the symbolic message that such exclusions send to established noncitizen populations can be alienating, effectively discouraging the sentiments of membership that would promote citizenship.

We believe that these concerns substantially outweigh the arguments offered in support of exclusion of presumptively permanent noncitizens from social benefits—a conclusion affirmed by most of the states in our study. Accordingly, we recommend that (1) access to welfare and other social benefits should be conditioned upon presumptive permanence and not citizenship; and (2) rights to residence should not be jeopardized by intermittent use of public benefits among presumptively permanent populations.

At the same time, however, we acknowledge that immigrants' sponsors should carry a time-limited support obligation for at least some cash and other benefit programs. But such obligations should not impose an open-ended fiscal liability on immigrants' sponsors, and they should not lead to gross disparities between the obligations imposed on the families of legal immigrants and those imposed on citizens. To illustrate, immigrants' sponsors should not be expected to finance the cost of providing health insurance to sponsored immigrants where extensive public programs exist for citizen populations.

### Rationing Access to the Labor Market on the Basis of Citizenship

Just as citizenship is rarely a prerequisite for receiving public benefits in the nations we examined, it is also rarely required for obtaining access to the work place or for undertaking self-employment. As a result, presumptively permanent noncitizens enjoy most of the same rights to work as citizens. Again, national policies vary more widely regarding the rights granted recently arrived or presumptively temporary immigrants. There are, however, important exceptions to these general trends.

#### Public Sector Employment

Citizenship still matters in the rationing of public sector jobs across virtually all the nations explored. Although blanket exclusions of noncitizens from civil service jobs have been invalidated by the courts in the United States (United States 1973), specific restrictions regarding positions deemed to be related to the exercise of state power have been upheld. This latter category includes public school teachers, state troopers, and probation officers (United States

1979; United States 1978; United States 1982). Along similar lines, France, restricts all railway, postal, and hospital jobs to EU citizens. Germany bars third-country nationals from all jobs in government service, including employment in public transportation and kindergarten (Vermeulen 1997). In countries where major economic sectors are administered by the government, the implications of reserving public sector jobs for citizens are more far reaching.

Two widely accepted rationales for restricting public sector employment are commonly advanced. Such policies are said to promote national security and to limit public policy decision making to full members of the state. And there are other rationales for limiting noncitizens' access to public employment that sweep far more broadly. These include giving noncitizens an incentive to naturalize or simply reserving a valuable public good for the citizenry.

Nonetheless, there are strong reasons to adopt more inclusionary policies regarding noncitizens' access to public sector jobs. From an instrumental perspective, it could be argued that noncitizens represent an expanding share of the total labor force and that their exclusion from the public sector restricts governments' access to a potentially rich labor pool. In an era of demographic change, it makes sense to include members of language and other minorities in the public service to promote better communication between communities of immigrant origin and police forces, public school faculties, licensing offices, and the like. Further, an inclusionary approach to public employment can promote a closer identitification of noncitizens with the state and the nation, rather than their withdrawal or exclusion from it. In some cases, this may require not just liberal hiring policies but that mainstream institutions make special accommodations.[60]

From an equity perspective, an argument made in support of noncitizen eligibility for public benefits applies to public sector employment as well: because noncitizens assume most of the societal obligations required of citizens, they should be eligible for most of the social and economic opportunities afforded by states to their citizens. Moreover, our proposal in chapter three that settled foreign nationals be granted the franchise at the local level suggests that immigrants are able to participate in the public sector—and surely in non-policy-related public employment.

On balance, then, we conclude that states that have blanket exclusions of noncitizens from public service jobs should rethink such policies. While it is reasonable to make exceptions for positions that implicate national security or high-level policy-making positions—just as it may be reasonable to ask high-level government officials to relinquish citizenship in another state—such exceptions should be closely circumscribed. Scant justification, for example, exists for limiting teaching positions in public schools to citizens.

*Private Sector Employment*

In most of the states we have examined, presumptively permanent noncitizens enjoy the same access to the private labor market as citizens. (These policies are catalogued in appendix I.) Our review also reveals that national policies generally do not encourage private employers to discriminate in favor of
citizens, and some states have express prohibitions on such discrimination.

Australia, Canada, the United Kindgom, and the United States offer striking
examples of open access from the time of admission to both the labor market
and self-employment. This access exceeds some of the most progressive,
inclusionary proposals contemplated for the EU.[61] As in the area of social welfare, these progressive policies in English-speaking states may be largely a
function of immigration rules, which admit immigrants as permanent residents
on track for citizenship rather than as temporary labor migrants.

There are, however, important exceptions to this overall pattern of comparatively inclusionary labor market policies. Although citizens from EU countries
enjoy free movement and open access to the labor markets in other EU countries, third-country nationals do not benefit from such rights; their rights to
residence and employment are generally defined by and limited to the EU state
that authorized their admission. In Germany, for example, family members of
third-country nationals who do not hold unrestricted residence or work permits
can be refused a labor permit if a German or EU citizen is available for the job.
In some German regions these family members—who will likely become long-
term, if not permanent, residents—can be excluded from all employment
(Groenendijk, Guild, and Barzilay 2001: 45). Moreover, access to the permanent residence status needed for free labor movement within Germany is limited by requirements that the applicant pass language tests and have a long
employment record.

Extensive restrictions on established noncitizen access to employment also
exist in Austria. Family members of third-country nationals can be excluded
from the labor market for a period of four to eight years. And the employment
rights of many established third-country nationals remain insecure, as they must
periodically renew their work permits and can be turned down depending on
patterns of labor market demand. Access to more secure jobs in the large, semi-
public sector is heavily influenced by political patronage, strong trade union
control, and citizenship requirements, which, taken together, virtually exclude
noncitizen workers.

Plainly, policies that facilitate the acquisition of nationality would open access to employment for third-country nationals within the EU. But other policies may also hold promise. In spring 2001, the European Commission issued a

directive proposing that after five years third-country nationals be allowed to work in EU states other than their country of residence.

Despite the comparative openness of the U.S. labor market, citizenship can still serve as a tie-breaker as employers can legitimately prefer a citizen over an "authorized alien" where the two are equally qualified for a job.[62] This legal defense may not only undermine the norms that reject alienage discrimination, but employers can also use it to cloak unauthorized discrimination on the basis of national origin or race. In contrast, preferring a citizen over a noncitizen in the case of two equal candidates for hire is unlawful under British and Dutch law. In practice, though, the use of citizenship as a "tie-breaker" has rarely been invoked in the United States. Thus, the provision stands as an anomaly against the backdrop of an antidiscrimination scheme that safeguards immigrants against citizenship discrimination in many circumstances.

Viewed from the perspective of promoting social and economic integration, such restrictive policies seem questionable. They withhold individuals from the labor market, and, presumably, government sponsored training for an extended period. During this period the immigrant's employment skills erode, only complicating later efforts to enter the labor market.

*Self-Employment*

Distinctions between citizens and noncitizens also arise in the area of self-employment. Noncitizens in France are barred from operating liquor or tobacco stores. In the United Kingdom, noncitizens who wish to operate their own business must demonstrate that they can provide employment for at least two persons already living in the country (Faist 2000). The economic significance of open access to self-employment should not be underestimated: Self-employed immigrants in the United States are the highest-paid class of all immigrant workers by a substantial margin (Fix and Passel 1994). Moreover, self-employment has a multiplier effect as many foreign-born workers (as well as native workers) in the United States and the United Kindgom work for immigrant entrepreneurs.

In summary, we note the general convergence among liberal democracies in not erecting citizenship as a barrier to private employment, self-employment, or public employment (except when the latter involves policy-formulation responsibilities). We believe that these represent wise policy choices and urge states to further scrutinize de facto and indirect restrictions on access to the labor market that raise obstacles to full economic participation of presumptively permanent immigrants.

### Is Citizenship Enough? Antidiscrimination Policies

As we noted in chapter three, the acquisition of citizenship rarely represents a point of completed political integration for an immigrant. The same is true as regards economic and social integration. Patterns of persistent disadvantage characterize some communities of immigrant origin within the nations we have examined. Thus, despite the fact that settled foreign nationals are generally afforded the economic and social rights granted citizens and despite the fact that naturalization guarantees all the rights of citizenship, it is plain that policies granting formal rights of access to social benefits and labor markets are not enough to bring about conditions of equality between native members of the host society and the visible minority groups that so frequently constitute communities of immigrant origin.

These facts raise broad questions of social policy well beyond the scope of this study. What we examine here is the place of antidiscrimination policy in a broader integration and citizenship agenda.[63]

It is clear that inclusionary welfare and work policies can be subverted by widespread discrimination in the labor market. Exclusion from the labor market will lead to exclusion from contributory social benefits such as social security and unemployment insurance that are tied to labor force participation.

Less obviously, discrimination will also lead to exclusion from the noncontributory social benefits that have become directly linked to work under the rules of the new welfare state. In the United States, for example, noncitizens can receive selected federal benefits if they can establish that they worked for forty quarters in formal employment. Several nations now link noncitizens' access to educational scholarships to either a parent's or the student's own employment history. By effectively making postsecondary education inaccessible, workplace discrimination not only disrupts the integration of the first-generation victim, it can also stall the integration of immigrants' children.[64] And, of course, discrimination in the labor market can defeat the goals of welfare-to-work programs as public funds spent on training are wasted and potential workers are demoralized.

Finally, as many social rights flow from private sector employment (health benefits, child care, and disability payments, for example), workplace discrimination denies noncitizens these integrating benefits as well.

The character and scope of each nation's antidiscrimination policies and enforcement efforts in Europe are detailed in John Wrench's study, *Preventing Racism at the Workplace: A Report on 16 European Countries* (1996). Here we will examine the experience of the United States, which has comparatively extensive antidiscrimination protections, enforcement regimes, and open labor markets, to see what lessons may be learned for immigrant integration policy.[65]

Recent research shows that, overall, second-generation workers aged twenty to thirty in the United States have incomes and wages comparable to third- and later-generation white, non-Hispanic immigrants (Passel and Van Hook 2000). There are, however, differences across groups. Asians in general do better than

whites, and Hispanics do worse. To the extent that second-generation noncitizen wages lag those paid to non-Hispanic whites, the difference can be almost
entirely accounted for by educational attainment.

Our review of the literature indicates that the persistence of disadvantage in
immigrant communities in Europe, however, cannot be as completely explained
by education levels and that discrimination may account for a larger share of
the second- and even third-generations' lagged economic progress (Wrench,
Rea, and Ouali 1999). Few EU states have a long tradition of detailed, comprehensive legislation forbidding racial discrimination. The United Kingdom and
the Netherlands are exceptions; both states have laws modeled after the first
generation of U.S. civil rights legislation. But even in these countries, sanctions
and enforcement agencies are comparatively weak. Further, systematic ethnic
registration and monitoring of employers is virtually absent in nearly all EU
countries. The Dutch positive action legislation of the early 1990s, which required the ethnic registration of workers, was highly controversial, largely un-
enforced, and did not produce strong, clear outcomes. This slow evolution of
antidiscrimination protections underscores the significance of the 2000 European Commission directive against racial discrimination that would oblige the
fifteen member states to adopt comprehensive antidiscrimination legislation by
mid-2003.[66]

The experience of the United States suggests elements of an effective antidiscrimination regime that are within the realm of political feasibility but that
are only selectively present in the EU member states. Such elements include:

(1)  Establishing administrative agencies that carry the right to impose civil
     sanctions for national origin as well as alienage discrimination and have
     the authority to initiate criminal prosecutions for serious and repeated
     offenses;
(2)  Granting a private right of action to aggrieved parties;
(3)  Providing inexpensive and ready access to a forum in which disputes
     can be heard and resolved; and
(4)  Financing extensive monitoring of changes in the character and ex-
     tent of discriminatory patterns—perhaps using the strategy of paired
     testing.

### Recommendations

As in chapter one, our policy recommendations here reflect a trend toward
convergence among liberal democracies. Importantly, states have generally
concluded that ensuring access to social benefits and labor markets for pre-

sumptively permanent foreign nationals does not undermine citizenship. Rather, such policies improve the chances of the kind of successful social and economic integration that ought to accompany full formal membership in a state. Specifically, we recommend:

(1) *Access to welfare and other social benefits should not be conditioned upon citizenship.* Rules restricting presumptively permanent foreign nationals from benefits are more likely to slow than to accelerate integration, and their provision will not diminish the importance of citizenship as a statement of civic engagement on the part of the individual. Presumptive permanence rather than citizenship should suffice for access to most benefits made available under the welfare state.

(2) *Neither rights to residence nor labor market security—nor rights to naturalization itself—should be jeopardized by intermittent use of public benefits among presumptively permanent foreign nationals.* Insecure residence and work rights for long-term residents are a self-evident barrier to integration.

(3) *Sponsor support obligations should not impose an open-ended fiscal liability on immigrants' sponsors and should not lead to gross disparities between the obligations imposed on the families of legal immigrants and those imposed on citizens.*

(4) *Employment policies, like welfare rules, should be constructed to promote integration of presumptively permanent residents. Hence citizenship should not be erected as a barrier to the labor market or to self-employment.* In practice this will mean that citizenship should generally not be a condition for the grant of professional licenses, for apprenticeships, or for entry into the civil service or the great majority of public sector jobs. This principle would not preclude limited exceptions for high-level governmental positions. The use of citizenship as a tie-breaker between equally qualified citizen and noncitizen candidates is problematic because it may complicate enforcement of bars against alienage and national-origin discrimination.

(5) *Antidiscrimination policies, coupled with an enforcement system that is carefully designed and adequately funded, can be an important tool in ensuring that rights of access to private employment are protected and in promoting social and economic equality for noncitizens and for citizens who are members of communities of immigrant origin.*

# Benefit Policies for Foreign Nationals in Selected Countries

Table A-1.  *Summary Table of Benefit Eligibility in Germany*

| Status | | Safety Net | | | | | Social Insurance | | Integration Assistance | Social Investments | | | Access to the Labor Market |
|---|---|---|---|---|---|---|---|---|---|---|---|---|---|
| | | Social Assistance (Sozialhilfe) | Housing Assistance — Rental Assistance | Housing Assistance — Social Housing | Child Assistance (Kindergeld) | Health Care and Insurance | Old Age Pension | Unemployment Insurance | | Grants or Loans for Higher Education | Education for Children | Job Training | |
| Citizen | German nationals | Yes | Yes | Yes | Yes | For employed, registered unemployed and their families | After being employed for a certain time | After being employed for a certain time | N/A | Yes | Yes | Yes | Open |
| Citizen | Ethnic Germans immigrants (*Aussiedler*) | Yes | Yes | Yes[b] | Yes | Yes | After being employed for a certain time | After being employed for a certain time | Yes | Yes | Yes | Yes | Open |
| Presumptively Permanent | Settled foreign nationals with unlimited residence permit[c] (*Aufenthaltsberechtigung*) | Yes[d] | Yes | Yes[e] | Yes[f] | For employed, registered unemployed and their families[g] | After being employed for a certain time (same as German citizens) | After being employed for a certain time (same as German citizens) | No | Yes | Yes | Yes | Open |
| Presumptively Permanent | Settled foreign nationals with limited residence permit[h] (*Aufenthaltserlaubnis*) | Yes[d] | Yes[f] | Yes[e] | Yes[f] | For employed, registered unemployed and their families[g] | After being employed for a certain time (same as German citizens) | After being employed for a certain time (same as German citizens)[i] | No | Yes | Yes | Yes | Restricted[j] |

| Group | Category | 1 | 2 | 3 | 4 | 5 | 6 | 7 | 8 | 9 | 10 | 11 | 12 |
|---|---|---|---|---|---|---|---|---|---|---|---|---|---|
| Presumptively Temporary | Recognized refugees (Asylberechtigte) | Yes | Yes | Yes | Yes | Yes | After being employed for a certain time (same as German citizens) | After being employed for a certain time (same as German citizens) | No | Yes | Yes | Yes | Open |
| | Asylum seekers and de facto refugees (Asylbewerber)[k] | Very Modest[l] | Yes | Yes[b] | No | Emergency care only | No | After being employed for a certain time (same as German citizens) | No | Yes | Yes | No | Very Limited[m] |
| | Temporary workers (project-tied or seasonal workers)[o] | No | No | No | No | Emergency care only[d] | No[o] | No[o] | No | No | No | No | Closed[m] |
| Supra-national | EU members[o] | Yes | Yes | No | Yes | Yes | Yes | Yes | No | Yes | Yes | Yes | Open |

*Sources:* Harald Waldrauch, "The Rights of Immigrants: Employment and Social Benefits: Tables Prepared for the Transatlantic Workshop on Citizenship and the Rights of Immigrants" (Vienna: European Centre for Social Welfare Policy and Research, 2000); Thomas Faist, "Rights and the Recognition of Immigrants in Welfare States: A Comparison of Institutional Conditions in Four European Countries," Institute for Intercultural and International Studies, University of Bremen, Bremen, Germany, 2000; Bryan Paul Christian, "Immigrant Welfare Entitlements in Cross-National Comparison: The Case of the United States and Germany," unpublished, 1998; Uwe Wenzel and Mathias Bös, "Immigration and the Modern Welfare State: The Case of the USA and Germany," *New Community,* Vol. 23, No. 4 (1997), pp. 537–48; Silvia Dörr and Thomas Faist, "Institutional Conditions for the Integration of Immigrants in Welfare States: A Comparison for the Literature on Germany, France, Great Britain, and the Netherlands," *European Journal of Political Research,* Vol. 31 (1997), pp. 401–26; Thomas Faist and Hartmut Häußermann, *Immigration, Social Citizenship, and Housing in Germany* (Abingdon, U.K.: Blackwell Publishers, 1996); Arne Gieseck et al., "Economic Implications of Migration into the Federal Republic of Germany, 1988–1992," *International Migration Review,* Vol. 29, No. 3 (1995), pp. 693–709. Additional information provided by Harald Waldrauch based on the following two volumes: Ulrike Davy, ed., "Die Integration von Einwanderern. Band 1: Rechtliche Regelungen im europäischen Vergleich" [The Integration of Immigrants, Volume 1: Comparing Legal Rules in European States] (Frankfurt, New York: Campus Verlag, 2001); and Harald Waldrauch, ed., "Die Integration von Einwanderern, Band 2: Ein Index der rechtlichen Diskriminierung" [The Integration of Immigrants, Volume 2: An Index of Legal Discrimination] (Frankfurt, New York: Campus Verlag, 2001).

[c] Child Assistance is only granted to those with certain types of residence permits (*Aufenthaltsberechtigung* or *Aufenthaltserlaubnis,* not *Aufenthaltsbewilligung* or *Aufenthaltsbefugnis*).

[b] Ethnic Germans have first preference in the pool of apartments in the social housing stock. Asylum seekers must be housed by local authorities while their asylum application is pending.

[c] This permit can be acquired at the earliest after 8 years of residence.

[d] Use of social assistance or even fulfilling the conditions for it (that is, lack of means) by noncitizens who have an ordinary (limited) permit (*Aufenthaltsbewilligung* and *Aufenthaltserlaubnis*) may result in nonrenewal of residence permit. But even for holders of an *Aufenthaltserlaubnis* the range of types of assistance to which they have a legal claim is limited; all other types of assistance may be granted "insofar as it is justified in the individual case at hand."

# Table A-1. Continued

[e]No discrimination against noncitizens with respect to access to publicly subsidized housing.

[f]Rental cash assistance or child assistance granted does not count as own income during the residence permit renewal process. Lack of sufficient income can lead to nonrenewal of the residence permit. In addition, no child assistance for children (of citizens or noncitizens) living abroad (unless provided for, on a reduced level, in bilateral agreements).

[g]No health insurance for family members (of citizens or noncitizens) living abroad (unless provided for in bilateral agreements).

[h]The so-called *Aufenthaltserlaubnis* may be a limited or an unlimited residence permit; in contrast, the *Aufenthaltsberechtigung* is always unlimited permit. An unlimited *Aufenthaltserlaubnis* can be acquired at the earliest after 5 years of residence. The so-called *Aufenthaltsbewilligung* is granted to persons whose residence is presumably temporary; holders of this title may not acquire a permanent residence right.

[i]If this worker is unemployed for more than one year and the Federal Employment Agency determines that the individual will not be able to find a job, the claim to unemployment insurance may be denied. EU members and Turkish nationals are not subject to this scrutiny.

[j]Restricted to occupation, occupational field, or contract. Holders of an unlimited *Aufenthaltserlaubnis* are free to take up any employment.

[k]If asylum proceedings take longer than one year, asylum seekers are entitled to benefits according to the federal law on welfare.

[l]Only asylum seekers and de facto refugees receive in-kind social assistance instead of cash assistance. Asylum seekers and de facto refugees receive a limited form of Aid to Subsistence while their asylum cases are processed. Since July 1, 1997, asylum seekers were given a time limit of three years for receipt of this form of assistance.

[m]Non-EU members can only accept a job if no German, EU member, or migrant with equal status can fill the position.

[n]Contract laborers may not claim social insurance benefits because they should be insured in their home country. However, they may claim emergency medical care, if necessary.

[o]EU members are included in the German welfare state as soon as they or their spouse enters the German labor market.

## Description of Benefit Programs in Germany

**Social Assistance** (*Sozialhilfe*)—Composed of Aid to Subsistence (legal claim) and Aid to Subsistence for Special Circumstances (granting of some types of assistance under this heading is based on the discretion of the authorities). Social assistance is means-tested cash assistance or assistance in-kind (for example, counsel, care, and others) for needy individuals.

**Rental Assistance** (*Wohngeld*)—Means-tested allowance used towards private rental or self-owned accommodations.

**Social Housing**—The state subsidizes the building of new houses that have to be rented out to persons whose income does not exceed certain limits. Ethnic Germans have priority in the queue for social housing. Asylum seekers must be housed by local authorities while their application for asylum is processed. If no public housing is available for asylum seekers, they may be housed in pensions/hotels, private-owned houses, public-owned buildings (for example, schools) or temporary accommodations. Costs are covered locally and are partly reimbursed by the Länder and the federal government.

**Child Assistance** (*Kindergeld*)—Cash allowance provided to families with children.

**Health Care and Insurance** (*Krankenversicherung*)—Contributory health care, usually provided through the employer. The government provides emergency health care to temporary workers and asylum seekers/de facto refugees.

**Old Age Pension** (*Rentenversicherung*)—Contributory pension for individuals in the labor force. Individuals may claim a government-provided old age pension after working a certain period of time.

**Unemployment Insurance** (*Arbeitslosenversicherung*)—Contributory insurance for individuals in the labor force. Individuals may claim this government-provided benefit when they are unemployed.

**Integration Assistance**—German language courses and retraining.

**Grants or Loans for Higher Education** (*Ausbildungsförderung*)—Grants for higher education financed by the state.

**Education for Children**—Public education.

**Job Training**—Vocational training provided by individual employers. Although subject to governmental regulation, employers decide who may obtain an apprenticeship so there is room for discrimination against noncitizens.

**Percentage of Foreigners in Total Population:** 8.9% (January 1, 1999)

Table A-2. Summary Table of Benefit Eligibility in Austria

| | Status | Safety Net | | | | Social Insurance | | | Social Investments | | | |
|---|---|---|---|---|---|---|---|---|---|---|---|---|
| | | Social Assistance (Sozialhilfe) | Housing Assistance | | Family Assistance (Familien-beihilfe) | Health Care and Insurance | Old Age Pension | Unemploy-ment Insurance | Grants or Loans for Higher Education | Educa-tion for Child-ren | Job Training | Access to the Labor Market |
| | | | Rental Assistance | Social Housing | | | | | | | | |
| Citizen | Austrian nationals | Yes | Yes | Yes | Yes | For employed, registered unemployed and their families | After being employed for a certain time | After being employed for a certain time | Yes | Yes | Yes | Open |
| Presumptively Permanent | Settled workers (noncitizens resident for more than 8 years) | Limited / local restrictions[a] | Limited / local restrictions[b] | Local restrictions[c] | Limited[d] | For employed, registered unemployed and their families[c] | After being employed for a certain time | After being employed for a certain time[f] | Limited[g] | Yes | Limited[h] | Restricted[i] |
| Presumptively Permanent | Other workers (noncitizens resident for less than 8 years) | Limited / local restrictions[a] | Limited / local restrictions[b] | Local restrictions[c] | Limited[d] | For employed, registered unemployed and their families[c] | After being employed for a certain time | After being employed for a certain time[f] | Limited[g] | Yes | Limited[h] | Restricted[i] |
| Presumptively Permanent | Recognized refugees | Yes | Yes | Yes | Yes | For employed, registered unemployed and their families | After being employed for a certain time | After being employed for a certain time | Yes | Yes | Yes | Open |
| Presumptively Temporary | Asylum seekers and de facto refugees | Limited / local restrictions[aj] | No[bk] | Limited / local restrictions[d] | No[d] | Limited[m] | No[n] | No[n] | No | Yes[o] | No | Severely restricted / no access[p] |
| Presumptively Temporary | Temporary workers: seasonal workers, harvesters, and "rotating" workers[aj] | Limited / local restrictions[aj] | No[bk] | No[r] | Limited[s] | Yes | Limited[t] | Limited[t] | No | Yes[o] | No | Restricted[u] |

continues

## Table A-2. Continued

| Status | Safety Net | | | | Social Insurance | | | Social Investments | | | |
|---|---|---|---|---|---|---|---|---|---|---|---|
| | Social Assistance (Sozialhilfe) | Housing Assistance | | Family Assistance (Familien-beihilfe) | Health Care and Insurance | Old Age Pension | Unemploy-ment Insurance | Grants or Loans for Higher Education | Educa-tion for Child-ren | Job Training | Access to the Labor Market |
| | | Rental Assistance | Social Housing | | | | | | | | |
| **Supra-national** — EU members | Yes | Yes | Yes | Yes | For employed, registered unemployed and their families | After being employed for a certain time | After being employed for a certain time | Yes | Yes | Yes | Open |

Sources: Harald Waldrauch, "The Rights of Immigrants: Employment and Social Benefits: Tables Prepared for the Transatlantic Workshop on Citizenship and the Rights of Immigrants" (Vienna: European Centre for Social Welfare Policy and Research, 2000); SOPEMI, *Trends in International Migration, 1999* (Paris: Organization for Economic Cooperation and Development, 1999). Additional information provided by Harald Waldrauch based on the following two volumes: Ulrike Davy, ed., "Die Integration von Einwanderern, Band 1: Rechtliche Regelungen im europäischen Vergleich" [The Integration of Immigrants, Volume 1: Comparing Legal Rules in European States] (Frankfurt, New York: Campus Verlag, 2001); and Harald Waldrauch, ed., "Die Integration von Einwanderern, Band 2: Ein Index der rechtlichen Diskriminierung" [The Integration of Immigrants, Volume 2: An Index of Legal Discrimination] (Frankfurt, New York: Campus Verlag, 2001).

[a] In 5 out of 9 regions, third-country nationals have access to social assistance only after 3-6 months, but even then they (like third-country nationals in a sixth region) are excluded from certain types of assistance (aid in special circumstances, social services, and some types of aid to subsistence) and in 3 out of the 5 they are not given a legal claim to aid to subsistence (like citizens). Continued use of social assistance may lead to nonrenewal of a residence permit or expulsion within the first 5 years of residence. Between 5 and 8 years, if there is no possibility of paying for own subsistence, nonrenewal of residence permit or expulsion may occur only in case the person is not willing and/or not able to earn his/her living. Only after 8 years of residence does the threat of nonrenewal of residence permit or expulsion desist.

[b] In 6 out of 9 provinces, third-country nationals are explicitly excluded from rental assistance; in the remaining 3 provinces, it is bound to additional criteria.

[c] Flats in houses built, bought, or renovated with public funds shall be rented out to persons whose income does not exceed certain limits. Noncitizens may be beneficiaries, but there is no rule of nondiscrimination to protect them so they may be excluded; most importantly, third-country nationals are explicitly excluded from access to subsidized flats owned by the municipality of Vienna (about one-fourth of all flats of Austria's capital). In addition, third-country nationals are excluded from subsidies for buying or building (sometimes even renovating) houses or flats in all nine provinces.

[d] Limited to noncitizens in the labor market or with 5 years of legal residence. In addition, no family assistance for children living abroad.

[e] Lack of health insurance may lead to nonrenewal of residence permit or expulsion within the first 5 years of residence. Between 5 and 8 years, if the person concerned does not have health insurance, nonrenewal of residence permit or expulsion may occur only in case the person is not willing and/or able to earn his/her living. Only after 8 years of residence does the threat of nonrenewal of residence permit or expulsion desist. In addition, there is no health insurance for family members (of citizens or noncitizens) living abroad (unless provided for in bilateral agreements).

[f] Noncitizens who have resided in Austria for more than 8 years are entitled to an unlimited benefit for long-term unemployed individuals.

[g] Third-country nationals are eligible for grants only if their parents were subject to income tax for 5 years in Austria, if they had the center of their life in Austria during this time and if they passed their school-leaving examination in Austria.

[h] First, nonemployed third-country nationals who may not be granted a work permit are not eligible for job trainings paid by the public employment office. A ministerial decree, though, has extended the groups of resident noncitizens who are eligible in principle for work permits and therefore also for job training courses considerably. Second, young noncitizens also need a work permit for taking on an apprenticeship. A considerable number of young persons did not fulfill the conditions for being granted a work permit every year until recently; the above mentioned decree also eased the conditions for being eligible for (at least the most restricted) work permit.

[f] Foreign workers are never completely exempted from the labor permit legislation. The best permit they can get is valid for 5 years, which is renewed if the individual maintained legal employment for 2.5 years in the past 5 years or for 5 years in the past 8 years. If they do not fulfill this condition, they (rather, their employer) may have to apply for a limited work permit (Beschäftigungsbewilligung), valid for a maximum of 1 year. The issue of this permit (not its renewal in case the job remains the same) is restricted by a quota.

[g] See note d above. In addition, social assistance is dependent on at least a provisional legal stay in most cases; only three provinces allow social assistance for persons with no right to stay under certain circumstances. The laws of three provinces state that social assistance for asylum seekers is only possible in case the person concerned does not have a claim to some assistance on the basis of some other law. Vienna explicitly denies asylum seekers a right to social assistance; assistance based on administrative discretion, though, is still possible.

[h] The question is irrelevant for asylum seekers, de facto refugees, seasonal workers, or harvesters in most cases.

[i] In addition, the federal state provides needy asylum seekers with accommodation, food, and health care but they do not have a legal claim to it. Fewer and fewer asylum seekers have been accepted into this program of federal support (Bundesbetreuung) in recent years. De facto refugees are granted accommodation, food, and health care.

[m] De facto refugees and asylum seekers in the program of federal support (see note l) do have access to health care; asylum seekers outside this program are dependent on emergency health care within the scope of social assistance.

[n] Normal conditions apply in case they are employed—which is highly unlikely (see column "access to the labor market").

[o] Compulsory education applies to all children who stay in Austria "permanently" and therefore also to children of asylum seekers, de facto refugees, and temporary workers who stay in Austria for more than just a few days or weeks. The law does not set legal residence as a condition.

[p] Asylum seekers need a labor permit, the issue of which is extremely unlikely as the authorities have to make sure that there are no workers available from 8 other groups of persons (citizens, recognized refugees, people with 8 years of residence, among others) who could fill the position. Up until the present, Austria gave protection to two groups of de facto refugees: Bosnians (1992–1995) and Albanians from Kosovo (1999–2000). Bosnians were given access to the regular system of employment of foreigners gradually, but they still needed a permit; Albanians were not given access to the labor market.

[q] Relevant groups in this context include: seasonal workers (maximum stay: 6 months), harvesters (maximum stay: 6 weeks), and employees of internationally operating companies who are designated to work in Austria only for a limited period of time (Rotationsarbeitskräfte); all other workers have the chance of making their stay a permanent one.

[r] See note h above. In addition, question is irrelevant for seasonal workers and harvesters.

[s] See note b above. In addition, seasonal workers and harvesters have no right to bring their families, and there is no family assistance for family members living abroad. Temporary workers in international companies do have the right to bring their families; in case they are employed (which is the basis of their residence permit), they may also get the benefit.

[t] Harvesters only have a mandatory health and accident insurance; seasonal workers and rotating workers also pay contributions to the old age pension and unemployment insurance, but they may be in the country for too short a period to be able to claim the benefits, which is the case for seasonal workers.

[u] The work permit of all three types of temporary workers is limited to a particular job.

### Description of Benefit Programs in Austria

**Social Assistance** (Sozialhilfe)—Consists of means-tested aid to subsistence, aid in special circumstances, and social services (types and forms of social assistance vary with province). It may be cash assistance or assistance in-kind (medical treatment, counsel, accommodation in special homes, care, among others). People who meet the conditions have a legal claim to aid to subsistence, whereas aid in special circumstances and social services are granted on a discretionary basis.

**Rental Assistance** (Wohnbeihilfe)—Means-tested allowance used toward private rental accommodations.

**Social Housing**—The provinces subsidize the building of new houses that have to be rented out to persons whose income does not exceed certain limits. De facto refugees as well as asylum seekers (in case they are accepted in the federal support program to which even asylum seekers with a provisional permit to stay do not have a legal claim) are granted accommodation.

**Family Assistance** (Familienbeihilfe)—Cash allowance provided to families with children.

**Health Care and Insurance** (Krankenversicherung)—Contributory health care linked to prior employment. However, poor people without health insurance may get health care as part of the system of social assistance.

**Old Age Pension** (Pensionsversicherung)—Contributory pension for individuals in the labor force. Individuals may claim an old age pension after having worked a certain period of time (15 years minimum) at the age of 60 (women) or 65 (men).

**Unemployment Insurance** (Arbeitslosenversicherung)—Contributory insurance for individuals in the labor force. Individuals may claim this benefit for 20 to 52 weeks when they are unemployed if they were employed for at least one (in case of first time unemployed) or one-half year (repeated unemployment). After the claim to unemployment benefit has been exhausted they have a claim to a different kind of benefit (Notstandshilfe) if they cannot pay for their subsistence.

**Grants or Loans for Higher Education**—Grants for higher education financed by the state.

**Education for Children**—Public education.

**Job Training**—(1) Courses provided by the public employment office (Arbeitsmarktservice) for registered unemployed to improve their skills and to enhance their employability; (2) apprenticeship: 3-year learning on the job at a specific employer, most often after leaving the Austrian school system at the age of 15.

**Percentage of Foreigners in Total Population: 9.1%** (Census, May 15, 2001)

**Percentage of Non-EU Citizens in Total Foreign Population: 84.9%** (Census, May 15, 2001)

Table A-3. *Summary Table of Benefit Eligibility in the Netherlands*

| | Status | Safety Net | | | | Social Insurance | | | | Social Investments | | | Access to the Labor Market |
|---|---|---|---|---|---|---|---|---|---|---|---|---|---|
| | | National Assistance | Housing Assistance | | Child Benefits | Health Care and Insurance[a] | Old Age[b] Pension | Unemployment Insurance | Integration Assistance | Grants or Loans for Higher Education | Education for Children | Job Training | |
| | | | Rent Subsidy | Social Housing | | | | | | | | | |
| Citizen | Dutch nationals | Yes | Yes | Yes | Yes | Yes | Yes | Yes | Yes | Yes | Yes | Yes | Open |
| Presumptively Permanent | Labor migrants, families | Yes | Yes | Yes | Yes | Yes | Yes | Yes | Yes | Yes | Yes | Yes | Open[c] |
| Presumptively Permanent | Recognized refugees and de facto refugees | Yes | Yes | Yes | Yes | Yes | Yes | Yes | Yes | Yes | Yes | Yes | Open |
| Presumptively Temporary | Asylum seekers | No[d] | No[d] | No[d] | No | Yes | No | No | No | No | Yes | No | Limited[e] |
| Presumptively Temporary | Temporary workers | Yes[f] | Yes | No | Yes | Yes | Yes | No | No | No | Yes | No | Closed[g] |
| Supra-national | EU members | Yes | Yes | Yes | Yes | Yes | Yes | Yes | No | Yes | Yes | Yes | Open |

Source: Harald Waldrauch, "The Rights of Immigrants: Employment and Social Benefits: Tables Prepared for the Transatlantic Workshop on Citizenship and the Rights of Immigrants" (Vienna: European Centre for Social Welfare Policy and Research, 2000); Thomas Faist, "Rights and the Recognition of Immigrants in Welfare States: A Comparison of Institutional Conditions in Four European Countries," Institute for Intercultural and International Studies, University of Bremen, Bremen, Germany, 2000; Silvia Dörr and Thomas Faist, "Institutional Conditions for the Integration of Immigrants in Welfare States: A Comparison for the Literature on Germany, France, Great Britain, and the Netherlands," *European Journal of Political Research*, Vol. 31 (1997), pp. 401–26. Additional information provided by Kees Groenendijk.

[a] Employers provide contributory health care and insurance for "normal risks." The government provides noncontributory health care for "special risks" (for instance, nursing home care).

[b] Old Age Pension is tied to employment indirectly. Individuals are paid, not based on contribution but on the basis of number of years present in the country during working age years (15-65). Any person legally resident in the Netherlands is entitled to a flat-rate pension above the minimum welfare level.

[f] For workers, access to the labor market is open after three years with a labor permit. For family members, access to the labor market is open directly after admission.

[j] Asylum seekers are excluded from almost all benefits. Almost all asylum seekers are housed in special government paid reception centers. Food and a small amount of pocket money is also provided to asylum seekers in these reception areas.

[c] After six months, asylum seekers may work seasonal jobs up to 12 weeks per year.

[d] Continued use of national assistance may lead to nonrenewal of residence permit.

[g] Temporary workers may only work on the basis of a labor permit restricted to a particular job with a particular employer. Only after three years will they have free access to employment.

**Description of Benefit Programs in the Netherlands**

**National Assistance**—Means-tested cash assistance for needy individuals.

**Rent Subsidy**—Means-tested allowance used toward private rental accommodations.

**Social Housing**—Placement in public authority housing.

**Child Benefits**—Cash allowance provided to families with children.

**Health Care and Insurance**—Classified into "normal risk" health care and "special risk" health care (for example, nursing home care), the government provides special risk health care to most individuals. Normal risk health care is contributory health care and insurance, usually provided through the employer.

**Old Age Pension**—Government-provided pension offered to elderly individuals based on the number of years legally present in the country during working age years (15-65).

**Unemployment Insurance**—Contributory insurance for individuals in the labor force. Individuals may claim this government-provided benefit when they are unemployed.

**Integration Assistance**—The 1998 Integration Act, *Inburgeringswet*, provides for an obligatory language and introduction course (600 hours) for most new immigrants.

**Grants or Loans for Higher Education**—Grants for higher education financed by the state.

**Education for Children**—Public education.

**Job Training**—A set of training measures provided by the government aimed at teaching special skills or improving access to employment for the participant.

**Percentage of Foreign-Born in Total Population:** 8.5% (January 1, 2000)

**Percentage of Noncitizens in Total Population:** 4.1% (January 1, 2000)

**Percentage of Non-EU Citizens in Total Noncitizen Population:** 69.9% (January 1, 2000)

Table A-4. *Summary Table of Benefit Eligibility in Canada*

| | Status | Safety Net | | | | | Social Insurance | | Social Investments | | | | Access to the Labor Market |
| | | Housing Assistance | | | Child Tax Benefit | Health Care and Insurance (provincial jurisdiction) | Old Age Security | Employment Insurance | Immigrant Settlement and Adaptation Program | Grants or Loans for Higher Education (provincial jurisdiction) | Education for Children (provincial jurisdiction) | Job Training | |
| | | Social Assistance (municipal jurisdiction) | Rent Subsidy | Social Housing (municipal & provincial jurisdiction) | | | | | | | | | |
|---|---|---|---|---|---|---|---|---|---|---|---|---|---|
| Citizen | Canadian nationals | Yes | Yes | Yes | Yes | Yes | Yes | Yes | N/A | Yes | Yes | Yes | Open |
| Landed immigrants (Presumptively Permanent) | Legal permanent residents (non-family class) | Yes[a] | Yes | Yes | Yes | Yes[b] | Yes[c] | Yes | Yes | Yes[d] | Yes | Yes | Open |
| | Family class legal permanent residents | No[e] | No[e] | No[e] | Yes | Yes[b] | Yes[c] | Yes | Yes | Yes[d] | Yes | Yes | Open |
| | Recognized refugees | Yes[a] | Yes | Yes | Yes | Yes[g] | Yes[c] | Yes | Yes | Yes[d] | Yes | Yes | Open |
| Nonpermanent residents (Presumptively Temporary) | Asylum seekers and de facto refugees | Yes | Yes | Yes (depending on region—municipal jurisdiction) | No | Yes[g] | No | Limited[h] | Yes | No | Yes | No | Restricted |
| | Temporary workers | — | — | — | Yes[i] | Yes[j] | No | Yes | Yes | No | Yes | No | Restricted |
| | Ministerial permit | Yes | Yes | Yes | No | Yes | No | Yes | Yes | No | Yes | Yes | Open |

Sources: Ravi Pendakur, "Canada," prepared for the Transatlantic Workshop on Citizenship and the Rights of Immigrants (Ottawa: Canadian Heritage, 2000); and Citizenship and Immigration Canada (CIC), "Welcome to Canada—What You Should Know: Basic Services," see <http://cicnet.ci.gc.ca/english/newcomer/welcome/wel-04e.html>.

[a] Social Assistance is administered at the provincial level and rules of eligibility may differ from province to province.

[b] Basic hospital and doctors' fees. In British Columbia, Ontario, and New Brunswick, noncitizens must wait 3 months before receipt of medical benefits.

[c] A reduced pension is provided to permanent residents living in the country for less than 40 years.

[d] Access to scholarships, bursaries, or student loans depend on length of residence in Canada.

[e] Sponsors of these immigrants sign a 10-year contract stating that the sponsor will be responsible for the food, clothing, and shelter of the sponsored immigrant and that the sponsored immigrant will not apply for social assistance. If they are found in violation of this contract, the sponsors may be taken to court for repayment and their ability to sponsor another relative is impaired.

[f] Refugees are also entitled to Resettlement Assistance (cash assistance) up to 12 months or until self-sufficient, whichever occurs first.

[g] Both recognized refugees and asylum seekers receive health benefits through the Interim Federal Health Program of Citizenship and Immigration Canada.

[h] In order to receive unemployment insurance, the recipient must have employment authorization. According to Citizenship and Immigration Canada (CIC), "only those who could not subsist without public assistance are eligible for employment authorization" (CIC 2000).

[i] Only those visitors or holders of a Minister's Permit who have lived in Canada for 18 months are eligible for the Child Tax Benefit.

[j] Temporary workers are granted medical benefits in select provinces.

## Description of Benefit Programs in Canada

**Social Assistance**—Means-tested cash assistance for needy individuals.

**Rent Subsidy**—Means-tested allowance used toward private rental accommodations.

**Social Housing**—Placement in public authority housing.

**Child Tax Benefit**—Federal government-provided monthly cash payments to parents or guardians of children under the age of 18. The amount differs according to family income, number of children, and ages.

**Health Care and Insurance**—Contributory health care, usually provided through the employer. The government provides emergency health care to all individuals. Eligibility rules differ by province.

**Old Age Security (OAS)**—Government-provided pension offered to elderly individuals based on the number of years legally present in the country after age 18.

**Unemployment Insurance**—Contributory insurance for individuals in the labor force. Individuals may claim this government-provided benefit when they are unemployed.

**Immigrant Settlement and Adaptation Program (ISAP)**—A federal government program that provides funds to immigrant-serving organizations. Quebec, Manitoba, and British Columbia do not use immigrant-serving organizations as an intermediary. Services provided with ISAP funds include:

(1) newcomer orientation;
(2) directing immigrants to community resources;
(3) providing interpretation or translation services;
(4) providing short-term counseling; and
(5) providing employment-related services.

**Grants or Loans for Higher Education**—Grants for higher education financed by the state.

**Education for Children**—Public education.

**Job Training**—Immigrant specific job training is handled by the Immigrant Settlement and Adaptation Program. All other job training is referred by local branches of Human Resource Centres of Canada (HRCC).

**Percentage of Foreigners in Total Population:** 18% (1996)

Table A-5. *Summary Table of Benefit Eligibility in the United States*

| | Status | | SSI | TANF | Food Stamps | State/Local Public Benefit | Rental Assistance | Public Housing | CHIP | Medicaid | Social Security | Unemployment Insurance | Loans and Grants for Higher Education | Education for Children | Job Training | Access to the Labor Market |
|---|---|---|---|---|---|---|---|---|---|---|---|---|---|---|---|---|
| | | | | | **Safety Net** | | Housing Assistance | | | | **Social Insurance** | | **Social Investment** | | | |
| Citizen | American nationals | | Yes | Yes | Yes | Yes | Yes | Yes | Yes | Yes | Yes | Yes | Yes | Yes | Yes | Open |
| Presumptively Permanent | Legal permanent residents | | No | Barred for first 5 years; state option afterward | No | State Option | Yes | Yes | Barred for first 5 years; eligible afterward | Barred for first 5 years; state option afterward | Yes | Yes | Yes | Yes | Yes | Open |
| | Legal permanent residents with 40 quarters of work[a] | | Barred for first 5 years; eligible afterward | Barred for first 5 years; state option afterward | Barred for first 5 years; eligible afterward | Eligible | Yes | Yes | Barred for first 5 years; eligible afterward | Barred for first 5 years; state option afterward | Yes | Yes | Yes | Yes | Yes | Open |
| | Recognized refugees | | Eligible for first 7 years | Eligible for first 5 years; state option[b] afterward | Eligible for first 7 years | Eligible for first 5 years; state option afterward | Yes | Yes | Yes | Eligible for first 7 years; state option[c] afterward | Yes | Yes | Yes | Yes | Yes | Open |
| Presumptively Temporary | Asylum seekers | | No | No | No | No[d] | Limited[e] | Limited[e] | No | No[f] | No | No | No | Yes | No | Restricted[g] |
| | Temporary workers (nonimmigrants) | | No | No | No | No[b] | Limited[e] | Limited[e] | No | No[f] | No | No | No | Yes | No | Restricted[h] |

*Note:* This table only applies to noncitizens who legally entered the United States after August 22, 1996. The eligibility of noncitizens who entered the United States before that date is less restricted than those who entered after but in many cases still not on par with citizens' eligibility.

Sources: National Immigration Law Center (NILC), "Overview of Immigrant Eligibility for Federal Programs," in *Building Immigrant Opportunities 2000—Public Benefit and Employment Strategies in the New Economy* (National Conference Binder) (Washington, D.C.: NILC, 2000); Wendy Zimmermann and Karen C. Tumlin, *Patchwork Policies: State Assistance for Immigrants Under Welfare Reform* (Washington, D.C.: Urban Institute, 1999); NILC, "Federal Laws and Implementation," in *Immigrants and Welfare Resource Manual: 1998 Edition* (Washington, D.C.: NILC, 1998).

[a] An immigrant may be credited with quarters of work completed by his/her spouse while married or parent while a minor child.
[b] Refugees are given Refugee Cash Assistance for their first 8 months in the United States if they do not qualify for TANF.
[c] Refugees are given Refugee Medical Assistance for their first 8 months in the United States if they do not qualify for Medicaid.
[d] State Option. States may provide state and local public benefits to unqualified immigrants only if they pass a law after August 22, 1996.
[e] Time limit of 18 months unless living with a citizen or a legal permanent resident.
[f] Emergency Care Only.
[g] Asylum seekers are barred from the labor market for 180 days. After this time period, employment authorization is subject to Immigration and Naturalization Service approval.
[h] Restricted to employer or occupational field.

## Description of Benefit Programs in the United States

**Supplemental Security Income (SSI)**—SSI is a needs-based program available to low-income individuals who are older than 64, blind, or disabled. SSI is monthly cash assistance that can be supplemented by state funds.

**Temporary Assistance for Needy Families (TANF)**—Cash payments, vouchers, social services, and other forms of assistance to low-income families with children.

**Food Stamps**—Coupons for low-income persons so that they may buy food at participating stores.

**State/Local Public Benefit**—These programs could include General Assistance or a similar cash assistance program for needy individuals and in-home assistance programs.

**Rental Assistance**—Vouchers and rental payments to landlords.

**Public Housing**—Housing in a publicly owned building. This can include rural housing for farmworkers.

**Child Health Insurance Program (CHIP)**—Health insurance coverage for uninsured, low-income children. Funding comes from the federal government but states design and implement the program.

**Medicaid**—Reimbursement for doctors' services, hospital care, and prescription drugs to participating providers who care for low-income persons. The federal government matches state funds for this program.

**Social Security**—Contributory pension for individuals in the labor force. Individuals may claim a government-provided old age pension after working a certain period of time.

**Unemployment Insurance**—Contributory insurance for individuals in the labor force. Individuals may claim this government-provided benefit when they are unemployed.

**Grants or Loans for Higher Education**—Grants for higher education financed by the state.

**Education for Children**—Public education.

**Percentage of Foreigners in Total Population:** 10% (1998)

Table A-6. *Summary Table of Benefit Eligibility in France*

| | Status | Safety Net | | | | | Social Insurance | | Social Investments | | | | Access to Labor Market |
|---|---|---|---|---|---|---|---|---|---|---|---|---|---|
| | | Social Assistance[a] | Housing Assistance | | Child Assistance | Health Care and Insurance | Old Age Pension | Unemployment Insurance | Integration Assistance | Education | Education for Children | Job Training | |
| | | | Rental Assistance | Public Housing | | | | | | | | | |
| Citizen | French nationals | Yes | Yes | Yes | Yes | Yes | Yes | Yes | Yes | Yes | Yes | Yes | Open |
| Presumptively Permanent | Migrants with permanent residence permit (*carte de résidence*) | Yes | Yes | Yes | Yes | Yes | Yes[b] | Yes | Yes | Yes | Yes | Yes | Open |
| | Migrants (including tolerated refugees) with long-term residence permit (*carte de séjour*)[c] | Yes | Yes | Yes | Yes | Yes | Yes[b] | Yes | Yes | Yes | Yes | Yes | Open |
| | Recognized refugees | Yes | Yes | Yes | Yes | Yes | Yes | Yes | Yes | Yes | Yes | Yes | Open |
| Presumptively Temporary | Asylum seekers | Limited[d] | No | No | No | No | No | No | Yes | No | Yes | No | Closed |
| | Temporary labor migrants and visitors | No | No | No | No | Restricted[e] | No | No | Yes | No | Yes | No | Limited |
| Supra-national | EU members[f] | Yes | Yes | Yes | Yes | Yes | Yes | Yes | Yes | Yes | Yes | Yes | Open |

Sources: Harald Waldrauch, "The Rights of Immigrants: Employment and Social Benefits: Tables Prepared for the Transatlantic Workshop on Citizenship and the Rights of Immigrants" (Vienna: European Centre for Social Welfare Policy and Research, 2000); Thomas Faist, "Rights and the Recognition of Immigrants in Welfare States: A Comparison of Institutional Conditions in Four European Countries," Institute for Intercultural and International Studies, University of Bremen, Bremen, Germany, 2000; SOPEMI, *Trends in International Migration, 1999* (Paris: Organization for Economic Cooperation and Development, 1999); Silvia Dörr and Thomas Faist, "Institutional Conditions for the Integration of Immigrants in Welfare States: A Comparison for the Literature on Germany, France, Great Britain, and the Netherlands," *European Journal of Political Research*, Vol. 31 (1997), pp. 401–26; Michael Bommes, Stephen Castles, and Catherine Wihtol de Wenden, "Post–1947 Migration to Australia and the Socio-Political Incorporation of Migrants," *Imis-Beiträge*, Vol. 13 (1999), pp. 13–42; William Rogers Brubaker, "Membership Without Citizenship: The Economic and Social Rights of Non-Citizens," in *Migration and Social Cohesion*, ed. Steven Vertovec (Cheltenham, U.K., and Northampton, Mass.: Edward Elgar, 1999), p. 262; Sami Naïr, "France: A Crisis of Integration," *Dissent*, Vol. 43 (Summer 1996), pp. 75–8; David M. Smith and Maurice Blanc, "Citizenship, Nationality, and Ethnic Minorities in Three European Nations," *International Journal of Urban and Regional Research*, Vol. 20 (1996), pp. 66–82.

[a]Although social assistance may be limited for adults, children receive some assistance irrespective of citizenship or nationality.

[b]France also provides contribution-independent increases for low pensions up to an old-age minimum, but these are limited to French citizens and nationals of countries who have signed agreements of reciprocity.

[c]Must be renewed every 10 years.

[d]Asylum seekers only have access to certain forms of cash assistance—they are eligible for fewer programs than are citizens and permanent residents.

[e]Only available to documented labor migrants—others have no access to health benefits and will be denied *carte de séjour* if an attempt is made to claim these benefits.

[f]These benefits are available to EU members who have joined the permanent labor force, not to visitors and travelers.

**Description of Benefit Programs in France**

**Social Assistance**—Means-tested cash payments to needy individuals.

**Rental Assistance**—Cash payments for assistance in paying rent.

**Public Housing**—Publicly owned and operated housing, now largely inhabited by immigrants.

**Child Assistance**—Means-tested cash payments to needy families with children.

**Health Care and Insurance**—French health care, following the insurance model, is contributory and tied to employment—thus nearly one million people are without health care, and it is assumed that immigrants are over-represented in this category. However, nongovernmental organizations generally fill these gaps.

**Old Age Pension**—Contributory pension for working individuals. The pension plan is progressive in that the government pays a minimum pension which is granted after 37.5 years of French residence regardless of place and citizenship—this favors low-income pensioners, a group in which immigrants are over-represented.

**Unemployment Insurance**—Contributory government-provided insurance for individuals in the labor force without a job.

**Integration Assistance**—French language instruction, available to those lacking appropriate French proficiency.

**Education**—Access to vocational school and higher education.

**Education for Children**—Public education.

**Job Training**—Government-sponsored classroom instruction and private training.

**Percentage of Foreigners in Total Population:** 5.6% (Census, March 8, 1999)

**Percentage of Non-EU Citizens in Total Foreign Population:** 63.4% (Census, March 8, 1999)

Table A-7. *Summary Table of Benefit Eligibility in the United Kingdom*

| | Status | Safety Net — Housing Assistance: Social Assistance | Safety Net — Housing Assistance: Rental Assistance | Safety Net — Housing Assistance: Public Housing | Safety Net: Child Assistance | Safety Net: Health Care and Insurance | Social Insurance: Old Age Pension | Social Insurance: Unemployment Insurance | Social Insurance: Integration Assistance | Social Investments: Education | Social Investments: Education for Children | Social Investments: Job Training | Access to Labor Market |
|---|---|---|---|---|---|---|---|---|---|---|---|---|---|
| Citizen | British nationals | Yes | Yes | Yes | Yes | Yes | Yes | Yes | Yes | Yes | Yes | Yes | Open |
| Presumptively Permanent | Migrants with permanent residence permits[a] | Five-year bar for third-country nationals; eligible otherwise | Five-year bar for third-country nationals; eligible otherwise | Five-year bar for third-country nationals; eligible otherwise | Five-year bar for third-country nationals; eligible otherwise | Yes | Yes | Yes | Five-year bar for third-country nationals; eligible otherwise | Yes | Yes | Yes | Open |
| Presumptively Permanent | Migrants with long-term residence permits[a] | Limited to certain[b] groups | Five-year bar for third-country nationals; eligible otherwise | Five-year bar for third-country nationals; eligible otherwise | Limited to certain[b] groups | Limited to certain[b] groups | Limited to certain[b] groups | Limited to certain[b] groups | Five-year bar for third-country nationals; eligible otherwise | Limited to certain[b] groups | Yes | Limited to certain[b] groups | Open |
| Presumptively Temporary | Recognized refugees | Yes | Yes[d] | Yes | Yes | Yes | Yes | Yes | Yes | Yes | Yes | Yes | Open |
| Presumptively Temporary | Asylum seekers | No[c] | Yes[d] | Yes[d] | No | Yes | No | No | Yes | No | Yes | No | Closed |
| Presumptively Temporary | Temporary labor migrants and visitors[a] | No | Yes[d] | Yes[d] | No | No | No | No | Yes | No | Yes | No | Limited[e] |
| Supra-national | EU members established as workers | Yes | Yes | Yes | Yes | Yes | Yes | Yes | Yes | Yes | Yes | Yes | Open |

Sources: Kees Groenendijk, Elspeth Guild, and Robin Barzilay, "The Legal Status of Third-Country Nationals Who Are Long-Term Residents in a Member State of the European Union" (Nijmegen, Netherlands: Centre for Migration Law, University of Nijmegen, 2001), see <http://www.jur.nl/cmr>; Harald Waldrauch, "The Rights of Immigrants: Employment and Social Benefits: Tables Prepared for the Transatlantic Workshop on Citizenship and the Rights of Immigrants" (Vienna: European Centre for Social Welfare Policy and Research, 2000); Thomas Faist, "Rights and the Recognition of Immigrants in Welfare States: A Comparison of Institutional Conditions in Four European Countries," Institute for Intercultural and International Studies, University of Bremen, Bremen, Germany, 2000; SOPEMI, *Trends in International Migration, 1999* (Paris: Organization for Economic Cooperation and Development, 1999); Lydia Morris, "Governing at a Distance: The Elaboration of Controls in British Immigration," *International Migration Review*, Vol. 32, No. 4 (1998), pp. 949–73; Silvia Dörr and Thomas Faist, "Institutional Conditions for the Integration of Immigrants in Welfare States: A Comparison for the Literature on Germany, France, Great Britain, and the Netherlands," *European Journal of Political Research*, Vol. 31 (1997), pp. 401–26.

[a] Temporary migrants, non-EU laborers, and family reunification migrants are admitted under the "no recourse to public funds condition," and thus these migrants are not eligible for public funds (the term *public funds* is understood to mean any type of social benefit, except for housing assistance, for which eligibility varies locally). Legislation passed in 1999 further extended the bar to third-country nationals admitted with "indefinite leave to remain" subject to a formal agreement that he or she will not have access to public funds for five years when they will be entitled to apply for naturalization.

[b] Only migrants granted an "indefinite/exception leave to remain" and resident for five years may receive these benefits.

[c] Local governments can grant up to 90% of social benefits to asylum seekers but it is up to their discretion.

[d] Subject to local variation.

[e] Limited to temporary labor migrants only.

## Description of Benefit Programs in Great Britain

**Social Assistance**—Means-tested cash payments to needy individuals.

**Rental Assistance**—Cash payments for assistance in paying rent.

**Public Housing**—Public authority housing units (council flats), distributed to needy families and individuals according to waiting lists, which can sometimes function to discriminate against immigrants.

**Child Assistance**—Means-tested cash payments to needy families with children.

**Health Care and Insurance**—The National Health Service (NHS) includes all residents regardless of individual contributions. Migrants admitted to the United Kingdom under the "no recourse to public funds" condition are denied the majority of public health benefits. However, the NHS runs special programs to address the needs of migrants or ethnic minorities.

**Old Age Pension**—Basic contributory flat-rate pension tied to payment of minimum contributions for set periods, combined with a contributory supplementary pension payment varying according to income.

**Unemployment Insurance**—Contributory government-provided pension for laborers without jobs.

**Integration Assistance**—English language instruction for those without appropriate English skills.

**Education**—Decentralized system of further education sponsored by the ministry of education and by several nongovernmental sources.

**Education for Children**—Public schools.

**Job Training**—Vocational training provided at colleges, although a larger emphasis is placed upon training by individual employers.

**Percentage of Foreign Nationals in Total Population:** 3.6% (1997)

## Table A-8. Summary Table of Benefit Eligibility in Australia

| | Status | Safety Net | | | | | Social Insurance | | | | Social Investments | | | | Access to Labor Market |
| | | Social Assistance | Housing Assistance | | Child Assistance | Parenting Payment | Health Care and Insurance (Medicare) | Disability Support Pension | Social Security | Old Age Pension | Integration Assistance | Education | Education for Children | Job Training | |
| | | | Rental Assistance | Public Housing | | | | | | | | | | | |
|---|---|---|---|---|---|---|---|---|---|---|---|---|---|---|---|
| Citizen | Australian nationals | Yes | Yes | Yes | Yes | Yes | Yes | Yes | Yes | Yes | Yes | Yes | Yes | Yes | Open |
| Presumptively Permanent | Migrants with permanent residence permit (Migration Stream) | Limited for first two years; eligible afterwards[a] | Limited for first two years; eligible afterwards[a] | Limited for first two years; eligible afterwards[a] | Yes | Yes | Limited for first two years; eligible afterwards[a] | Yes | Limited for first two years; eligible afterwards[a] | 10 year residency requirement, eligible afterwards | Yes | Limited for first two years; eligible afterwards[a] | Yes | Yes | Open |
| Presumptively Permanent | Recognized refugees (Humanitarian Stream) | Yes | Yes | Yes | Yes | Yes | Yes | Yes | Yes | Yes (may be waived from residency requirement) | Yes | Yes | Yes | Yes | Open |
| Presumptively Temporary | Asylum seekers with bridging visa | Yes[b] | Yes | Yes | Yes | No | Yes | No | Yes | No | Yes | No | No | No | Limited[c] |
| Presumptively Temporary | Asylum seekers without a bridging visa | No | No | No | No | No | No | No | No | No | No | No | No | No | No |
| Presumptively Temporary | Temporary workers and visitors (Economic, Socio/Cultural, and International Relations Streams) | Yes[c] | Yes[c] | Yes[c] | Yes[c] | No | Yes[c] | No | Yes[c] | Yes[c] | Yes | Yes | Yes | Yes | Limited[d] |

Sources: Australian Bureau of Statistics, "Australia Now: A Statistical Profile (Population)," 2000, see <http://abs.gov.au>; Australian Department of Immigration and Multicultural Affairs, "Help for Migrants and Refugees Settling in Australia," Commonwealth of Australia, November 28, 2000, see <http://www.immi.gov.au>; Allan Borowski, discussion presented at the Transatlantic Workshop on Citizenship and the Rights of Immigrants, European University Institute, Florence, Italy, April 2–4, 2000, and subsequent conversations; Centrelink,"Services for People with Special Needs," 2000, see <http://centrelink.gov.au/internet/internet.nsf/services/index.htm>; Gianni Zappalà and Stephen Castles, "Citizenship and Immigration in Australia," in *From Migrants to Citizens: Membership in a Changing World*, ed. T. Alexander Aleinikoff and Douglas Klusmeyer (Washington, D.C.: Carnegie Endowment for International Peace, 2000); Michael Bommes, Stephen Castles, and Catherine Wihtol de Wenden, "Post–1947 Migration to Australia and the Socio-Political Incorporation of Migrants," *Imis-Beiträge*, Vol. 13 (1999), pp. 13–42; Jill Murphy and Lynn Williams, "Social Security Recipiency Among Recently Arrived Immigrants," *People and Place*, Vol. 4, No. 2 (1996) (electronic journal); Bob Birrell and Samantha Evans, "Recently Arrived Migrants and Social Welfare," *People and Place*, Vol. 4, No. 2 (1996) (electronic journal); Ernst Healy, "Welfare Benefits and Residential Concentrations Amongst Recently Arrived Migrant Communities," *People and Place*, Vol. 4, No. 2 (1996) (electronic journal); Siew-Ean Khoo, "Correlates of Welfare Dependency Among Immigrants in Australia," *International Migration Review*, Vol. 28, No. 1 (1994), pp. 68–90. Additional information provided by Allan Borowski of Latrobe University.

[a]Migrants in the Migration Stream category must have been sponsored by a citizen or permanent resident who will post an "Assurance of Support" bond which will repay certain benefits claimed during the migrant's first two years of residence in Australia.

[b]Not available to all asylum seekers; in some cases eligibility is dependent upon the type of bridging visa granted.

[c]These migrants are only eligible to claim these benefits following a two-year waiting period.

[d]Not open to temporary visitors.

**Description of Benefit Programs in Australia**

**Social Assistance**—Means-tested cash payments to needy individuals and immigrants who have passed the two-year waiting period.

**Rental Assistance**—Allowance toward private rental accommodations.

**Public Housing**—Publicly owned housing units available for the poor.

**Child Assistance** (Family Assistance)—Cash payments provided to families with children.

**Parenting Payment**—Cash assistance provided to individuals who become single parents.

**Health Care and Insurance** (Medicare)—Contributory health services available to all, although migrants must fulfill two-year residency requirement.

**Disability Support Pension**—Available to immigrants if the inability to work due to physical, intellectual, or psychiatric impairment occurred after arriving in Australia.

**Social Security**—Means-tested flat-rate categorical income support system for the unemployed and elderly.

**Age Pension**—Means-tested old age pension. All claimants/applicants must be Australian residents for at least ten years. Those who arrived in Australia as refugees or under a special humanitarian program may be exempted from the residency requirement.

**Integration Assistance**—English language tuition for immigrants older than 18 years and with insufficient English abilities.

**Education**—Grants for state-sponsored higher education, generally through the Austudy program.

**Education for Children**—Public education.

**Job Training**—Vocational training provided by the state and individual employers.

**Percentage of Foreign-Born in Total Population: 23%** (June 1998)

Table A-9. *Summary Table of Benefit Eligibility in Israel*

| | | Safety Net | | | | Social Insurance | | | Social Investments | | | | Access to Labor Market |
| | | Housing Assistance[a] | | | | | | | | | | | |
| Status | | Social Assistance | Rental Assistance | Public Housing | Child Assistance | Health Care and Insurance[b] | Old Age Pension | Unemployment Insurance | Integration Assistance | Education | Education for Children | Job Training | |
|---|---|---|---|---|---|---|---|---|---|---|---|---|---|
| Citizen | Law of Return citizens[b] | Yes | Yes | Yes | Yes | Yes | Yes | Yes | Yes | Yes | Yes | Yes | Open |
| | Naturalized citizens[c] | Yes | Yes | Yes | Yes | Yes | Yes | Yes | Yes | Yes | Yes | Yes | Open |
| Presumably Permanent | Migrants with temporary residence cards | Yes | Yes | Yes | Yes | Yes | Yes | Yes | Yes | Yes | Yes | Yes | Open |
| Presumably Temporary | Recognized refugees[e] | Yes | — | Yes | Yes | Yes | Yes | Yes | Yes | Yes | Yes | Yes | Open |
| | Asylum seekers[f] | — | — | — | — | — | — | — | — | — | — | — | — |
| | Temporary work migrants | No | No[g] | No[g] | No | No[gh] | No | No | No | No | Yes | No[g] | Limited[i] |

[a] In addition to these forms of housing assistance, new immigrants are eligible to receive low-interest state-supported mortgages.

[b] Law of Return citizens are Jewish migrants or migrants directly related to Jews who are invited to settle in Israel; they are immediately granted citizenship, based upon the *jus sanguinis* principle.

[c] Naturalized citizens are non-Jewish immigrants who must meet certain criteria for citizenship, including a residency requirement and renunciation of prior citizenship—two important requirements that Jews are not required to meet.

Sources: Allan Borowski, discussion presented at the Transatlantic Workshop on Citizenship and the Rights of Immigrants, European University Institute, Florence, Italy, April 2–4, 2000, and subsequent conversations; Central Bureau of Statistics, Israel, "Statistical Abstract of Israel: Population," March 6, 2000, see <http://www.cbs.gov.il/shnaton51/shnatone51.htm>; Zeev Rosenhek, "Migration Regimes, Intra-State Conflicts and the Politics of Exclusion and Inclusion: Migrant Workers in the Israeli Welfare State," paper presented at the Third International Metropolis conference, 1998; Ayelet Shachar, "Citizenship and Membership in the Israeli Polity," in *From Migrants to Citizens: Membership in a Changing World*, ed. T. Alexander Aleinikoff and Douglas Klusmeyer (Washington, D.C.: Carnegie Endowment for International Peace, 2000), pp. 386–433; Ian S. Lustick, "Israel as a Non-Arab State: The Political Implications of Mass Immigration of Non-Jews," *Middle East Journal*, Vol. 53, No. 3 (1999), pp. 417–33; Iris Geva-May, "Immigration to Israel: Any Lessons for Canada?" paper presented at Research on Immigration and Integration in the Metropolis (RIIM) conference, Vancouver, Canada, 1996; Fran Markowitz, "Living in Limbo: Bosnian Muslim Refugees in Israel," *Human Organization*, Vol. 55, No. 2 (1996), pp. 127–32. Additional information provided by Allan Borowski of Latrobe University and John Gal and Uri Yanay of the Paul Baerwald School of Social Work, Hebrew University, Jerusalem.

[d] Temporary residence status last three years, at which point temporary residents must decide to become naturalized citizens or to leave the country.

[e] This category only serves to identify non-Jewish refugees, as Jewish refugees, by virtue of their *jus sanguinis* privilege, are part of the aggregate of Law of Return citizens. Similar to the asylum seekers (see note f), it seems that refugees do not have an official status of their own; rather they are admitted on tourist visas but are somehow recognized as refugees. There are very few noncitizens who fall into this category.

[f] It would appear that asylum seekers enter on tourist visas and are not granted special status—this holds only for non-Jewish asylum seekers, as all Jews immediately achieve citizenship as stipulated by the Law of Return. The process for non-Jewish asylum seekers, however, is unclear, as it appears that those non-Jewish migrants who are essentially asylum seekers do not have an official and discrete status under the Israeli migration regime. There are very few noncitizens who fall into this category.

[g] The provision of these benefits is the responsibility of private employers.

[h] According to a recently passed law, children of temporary workers are now eligible for health care.

[i] Limited only to specific jobs for which these migrants were recruited; upon termination of employment, these migrants are required to leave the country.

**Description of Benefit Programs in Israel**

**Social Assistance**—Cash payments for needy individuals.

**Rental Assistance**—Allowance for use in private accommodations.

**Public Housing**—Government owned and run housing.

**Child Assistance**—Cash allowance provided to families with children.

**Health Care and Insurance**—Contributory state-run health insurance open to all citizens. Health care for temporary workers, however, is the responsibility of the employers, although little action has ever been taken by the state to ensure that employers provide health care.

**Old Age Pension**—Contributory pension for elderly workers.

**Unemployment Insurance**—Government-provided insurance offered to laborer-citizens without jobs (noncitizen laborers must leave the country upon termination of employment).

**Integration Assistance**—Hebrew instruction through the *ulpan* system.

**Education**—State-subsidized higher education.

**Education for Children**—Public schools.

**Job Training**—Vocational training provided by the state and by individual employers; noncitizen laborers must be trained by their employers only.

**Percentage of Foreign-Born in Total Population:** 38.7% (1998 Average)

# Comparative Citizenship Project*
# Working Group Participants

**Project Codirectors**

T. Alexander Aleinikoff
Professor
Georgetown University Law Center
Senior Policy Analyst
Migration Policy Institute
United States

Douglas Klusmeyer
Assistant Professor, Department of Justice, Law and Society
American University
Visiting Fellow
Migration Policy Institute
United States

**Access to Citizenship**

Patrick Weil (Chair)
Professor, Department of History
University of Paris Sorbonne
France

---

*A project of the Carnegie Endowment's International Migration Policy Program, which became the Migration Policy Institute in September 2001.

Joseph Carens
Professor, Department of History
University of Toronto
Canada

Miriam Feldblum
Senior Research Fellow
Division of Humanities and Social Sciences
California Institute of Technology
United States

Christian Joppke
Professor, Department of Political and Social Sciences
European University Institute
Florence, Italy

André Liebich
Professor, International History
Graduate Institute of International Studies
Geneva, Switzerland

Judge Rui Moura Ramos
Professor, Faculty of Law
University of Coimbra
Portugal

Peter Schuck
Simeon E. Baldwin Professor of Law
Yale University Law School
United States

Audrey Singer
Visiting Fellow
Center on Urban and Metropolitan Policy
The Brookings Institution
United States

**Dual Nationality**

David Martin (Chair)
Professor
University of Virginia School of Law
United States

Kay Hailbronner
Professor
University of Konstanz
Germany

Antonia Hernandez
President and General Counsel
Mexican American Legal Defense and Educational Fund
Los Angeles, California
United States

Karen Knop
Professor, Faculty of Law
University of Toronto
Canada

Ruth Rubio Marin
Professor, Constitutional Law
University of Seville Faculty of Law
Spain

**Political Participation**

Rainer Bauböck (Chair)
Professor
Austrian Academy of Sciences
Vienna, Austria

Will Kymlicka
Professor, Department of Philosophy
Queens University
Canada

Marco Martiniello
Researcher and Head of Conferences
Department of Political Science
University of Liege
Belgium

Tariq Modood
Professor, Department of Sociology
University of Bristol
United Kingdom

David Scobey
Assistant Professor, Architecture
Director, Arts of Citizenship Program
College of Architecture and Urban Planning
University of Michigan
United States

Aristide Zolberg
Visiting Fellow
Russell Sage Foundation
United States

## Social and Economic Rights

Michael Fix (Chair)
Director, Immigration Studies Program
The Urban Institute
United States

Adrian Favell
Associate Professor, Department of Sociology
University of California, Los Angeles
United States

Kees Groenendijk
Professor, Center for Migration Law
University of Nijmegen
The Netherlands

Riva Kastoryano
Researcher to CNRS, CERI
National Foundation for Political Science
France

Susan Martin
Director, Institute for the Study of International Migration
Georgetown University
United States

# *Notes*

## Chapter One: Access to Citizenship

1. In this study, we use the terms *citizenship* and *nationality* interchangeably, with full awareness that the domestic laws of some states draw important distinctions between the two concepts.

2. This importance is reflected in core international human rights principles. See the Universal Declaration of Human Rights, article 15: (1) Everyone has the right to a nationality; and (2) No one shall be arbitrarily deprived of his nationality nor denied the right to change his nationality (United Nations 1948).

3. In chapter three, we recommend that settled foreign nationals be granted franchise rights at the local level.

4. This categorization does not address questions about the status of children who are born in the country of immigration or who arrive at an early age, but who return to their parents' country of origin for some portion of their formative years. Some of the questions that might be asked about such children will be addressed implicitly below.

5. These policies are sometimes referred to as "double *jus soli*," a phrase we find misleading. We will label such policies "third-generation birthright citizenship."

6. It also worth noting that states with strict rules prohibiting the naturalization of persons convicted of criminal offenses may preclude members of this class from citizenship for acts undertaken as juveniles or young adults.

7. This is not necessarily true for states such as Canada and the United States that admit large numbers of immigrants for permanent residence who have not previously resided in the country.

8. We recommend below that renunciation requirements not be required for naturalization (see chapter two). We believe that the arguments for a renunciation requirement in the German context are even weaker, both because the child granted citizenship at birth will have undergone a socialization process in the country of residence and because it will mean that persons who have already enjoyed full citizenship rights (including the franchise) in their country of residence will be stripped of those rights should they want to retain their second citizenship.

9. France, in former years, required individuals to register for acquisition of status. Many eligible persons failed to do so, believing that they already possessed French nationality.

10. What residence means legally and to what extent it actually requires one's physical presence in the country is something that could only be determined by a more careful examination of administrative and legal practice than we have been able to undertake, but it is safe to assume that the vast majority of foreign nationals who become citizens in these countries actually live there most of the time.

## Chapter Two: Managing Dual Nationality

11. See, for example, Decision of 21 April 1974, Entscheidungen des Bundesverfassungsgerichts [BverfGE] 37, 217 (254-55) (F.R.G.); and United States (1972).

12. On January 3, 2000, the convention entered into force with three parties (Austria, Moldova, and Slovakia); seventeen other states have signed but not yet ratified the treaty.

13. Nationality Act, § 4(3) (Staatsangehörigkeitsgesetz, StAG), v. 22.7.1913 (RGBl. I S.583), as last amended by Act of 23 July 1999, v. 23.7.1999 (BGBl. I S.1618). These provisions took effect January 1, 2000. Section 29 of the same act, also added in 1999, requires that a person who acquires German citizenship in this fashion choose between ages eighteen and twenty-three which single nationality he or she wishes to keep. This election requirement will be discussed below.

14. U.S. statistics are illustrative of this trend. From 1991 to 1997, the number of immigrant admissions of foreign spouses of U.S. citizens grew from 125,397 to 170,263, a 35 percent increase (INS 1999: 32).

15. International treaties have also targeted such discrimination (United Nations 1957, 1979).

16. Germany has not signed or ratified the 1997 European Convention on Nationality (Council of Europe 1997).

17. The fountainhead 1947 Canadian Citizenship Act contained no renunciation requirement. Canada continued this policy in the comprehensive revision that resulted in the 1977 Citizenship Act [see § 5(1)], which also went further and eliminated a provision that had decreed loss of Canadian citizenship for its nationals who naturalized elsewhere (Galloway 2000). Australia in 1986 deleted the requirement that naturalizing citizens renounce their former nationality (Zappalà and Castles 2000: 46–7).

18. See Agreement on Nationality, Spain-Colombia (United Nations 1979) and Agreement on Dual Nationality, Spain-Bolivia (United Nations 1961).

19. For a comprehensive description, see Legomsky (2002).

20. Annex 23 to the 1907 Hague Convention Respecting the Laws and Customs of War forbids a state from compelling an individual, whether mono-national or dual national, to take up arms against a country of nationality (Scott 2000: 368, 389). This principle is generally considered to have attained the status of customary international law. But individuals may still volunteer to participate in the wartime effort, and treason convictions in the other nation following the war have sometimes resulted (Legomsky 2002).

21. See the Nottebohm Case, which speaks of the "general aim of making the legal bond of nationality accord with the individual's genuine connection with the State," and observes that "nationality is a legal bond having as its basis a social fact of attachment, a genuine connection of existence, interests and sentiments, together with the existence of reciprocal rights and duties" (International Court of Justice 1955).

22. These conditions mirror those set forth in Article 15(2) of the Universal Declaration of Human Rights: "No one shall be arbitrarily deprived of his nationality nor denied the right to change his nationality" (United Nations 1948).

## Chapter Three: Citizenship Policies and Political Integration

23. Among these are Austria, Germany, and Switzerland. In France such legal restrictions were lifted only in 1981.

24. This restriction exists in some Central Eastern European states, for example in Poland and Romania. Article 2 of the German Law on Political Parties does not recognize associations as political parties if a majority of either their members or their directorates are foreign nationals.

25. Historically, voting was not always strictly tied to nationality. For example, throughout the nineteenth century and into the early twentieth century, a number of states in the United States granted the franchise to certain classes of noncitizens.

26. Extension of the franchise should never be regarded as a substitute for easier access to nationality. For reasons spelled out in chapter one, promoting access to citizenship serves important integrative functions irrespective of the formal rights that immigrants enjoy. Granting the franchise while maintaining barriers to full membership sends a message of exclusion, not inclusion.

27. A case can be made that granting the franchise for the European Parliament to nationals of other member states is tied to the project of creating a supranational citizenship of the union. Exclusion of third-country nationals would then be less problematic. However, as we have argued above, making the franchise an exclusive privilege of citizenship is legitimate only if immigrants can gain access to citizenship. For the EU, this would require a liberalization and harmonization of the nationality laws of member states that determine also the admission to EU citizenship. For the local franchise there is no such justification for excluding third-country nationals. Municipal authorities are not institutions of the union; they must be accountable to the local resident population independently of its national origin.

28. In May 2000 two municipalities in Jura voted to introduce noncitizen eligibility for local office.

29. The convention has been put into force by Italy, the Netherlands, Norway, and Sweden. Cyprus, Denmark, Finland, and the United Kingdom have signed the treaty but have not yet put it into force. Italy has, however, not acceded to that part of the convention that contains the provision on voting rights.

30. In a few countries (such as Switzerland), free internal movement for noncitizens is restricted through residence permits that are only valid within a part of the territory. More commonly, free movement is limited through work permits that tie immigrants to a specific employer or permit a change of jobs only within a certain province or economic sector.

31. A notable exception here is jury service in the United States, which is a local obligation imposed only on citizens.

32. In Sweden, noncitizen residents vote not only in local elections but also in regional ones and in referenda. The first national referendum with immigrant participation was held in 1980 on the issue of nuclear power. In the Swiss canton Jura, noncitizens may vote in plebiscites except those that concern constitutional issues.

33. The German Constitutional Court suggested this argument in 1990 when it invalidated legislation in Hamburg and Schleswig-Holstein that would have introduced voting rights for noncitizens at the level of state elections in the former and a local franchise based on reciprocity in the latter. The court also pointed out that the constitutional path toward a more inclusive franchise was to reform the German nationality law (see BVerfGE 83, 37 und BVerfGE 83, 60).

34. There are, however, instances of local voting rights without specific residence requirements for noncitizens (for example, the local franchise in Ireland or local voting rights for EU citizens in other member states).

35. For example, in Sweden, foreign nationals acquire the local and regional franchise after three years of legal residence and can be naturalized after five years.

36. Our argument presupposes that the transition to permanent residence status does not depend on a discretionary decision by immigration authorities but is completed automatically after a fixed number of years of legal residence.

37. With the exception of residents of New York City, foreign citizens in the United States generally cannot participate in elections of school boards. In Austria, foreign nationals may vote, but only those from EU member states or countries with association agreements can run as

candidates in elections for works councils, student parliaments, or chambers of labor (in which membership is compulsory).

38. Among our project countries, Australia, Belgium, Greece, Italy, and Luxembourg have compulsory voting.

39. Statistical calculations of participation rates may sometimes be quite misleading. In elections where noncitizens enjoy a franchise, low voting rates need not indicate a general lack of political interest among ethnic minorities. One of the factors that contributes to lower rates among foreign nationals in local elections in Scandinavia or the Netherlands is that noncitizens who are more likely to vote are also more likely to naturalize. Naturalizations may thus diminish the pool of active voters and even more so of potential candidates among noncitizens.

40. Western democracies have quite different traditions of direct or indirect public support of activities in civil society that contribute to public policy goals. European countries often directly subsidize such activities whereas in the United States they are supported through tax exemptions. We do not want to suggest that one model is preferable to the other, but merely that associations providing useful services to communities of immigrant origin should be covered by available means of support.

41. Foreign-born voters can still have a decisive impact under majoritarian voting where they are regionally concentrated (as they are, for example, in Southern California) and where swing votes decide the outcome.

42. This effect results, on the one hand, from naturalizations and, on the other hand, from the demographic structure of most immigrant populations who are generally younger than the native average.

43. These points are included in the 1998 Charter of European Parties for a Non-Racist Society, which has been signed by nearly one hundred parties including conservative, liberal, social democratic, and environmentalist ones.

## Chapter Four: Social Rights and Citizenship

44. Zlotnick (1998) assessed international migration trends in five countries included in our analysis—Australia, Canada, Germany, the Netherlands, and the United States.

45. EU citizens who do not have a job must have sufficient income and private health insurance to cover their stay in another member country.

46. Tomas Hammar (1989) labels this class of settled foreign nationals who are generally eligible for most social and economic rights as "denizens."

47. In strictly *jus soli* nations such as the United States and Canada, however, the citizen children of undocumented immigrants are eligible for the full range of benefits, creating tiers of eligibility within one family. The consequences for these "mixed" status households are particularly distressing when social rights are rationed based on citizenship (Fix and Zimmerman 1999).

48. This strong central tendency among the nations studied has led us away from attempting to rank them on the basis of the relative inclusiveness of their rights regimes. Such a ranking would be more meaningful for temporary than for established immigrants.

49. Of course, there may be substantial movement from temporary to permanent legal status in the United States among students, workers, and even visitors as attachments deepen, marriages form, and permanent jobs are found.

50. As Rogers Brubaker (1999: 262) writes, "Thus the status of permanent resident alien in the United States and landed immigrant in Canada is roughly similar to that of persons with 'indefinite leave to remain' in the United Kingdom, of persons with 'right to residence' (*Aufenthaltsberechtigung*) in the Federal Republic of Germany, of persons with the 'Carte de Resident' in France."

51. Certain factors such as marriage to a citizen, family reunification, and refugee status can speed up the transition from a temporary noncitizen to a presumptively permanent foreign national, and thus access to public benefits.

52. The time from entry to the grant of established status can range widely from a matter of months (often the case in France) to ten years or more (occasionally the case in France). The transition can be conditioned upon the issuance of multiple temporary permits of short duration (Austria) or a single administrative approval (France).

53. The Immigration and Asylum Act 1999 encountered significant legal barriers soon after enactment. A judgment issued on June 22, 2000, in the cases of *O v. London Borough of Wandsworth* and *Bhikha v. Leicester City Council* ruled that social service agencies should not consider immigration status when assessing an individual client's need for assistance under § 21 National Assistance Act 1948 (amended by § 116 Immigration and Asylum Act 1999). Shifting the burden of determining immigrant status back to the Secretary of State, the ruling stated that local social service authorities did not have the authority to "starve immigrants out of the country by withholding last resort assistance" (United Kingdom 2000b).

54. For temporary immigrants, the threat of loss of work and residence permits in Germany is much more real.

55. In Canada sponsors are required to offer support for ten years and in Australia for two years. No fixed term of years is set for the United States, where an immigrant must work for forty quarters in covered employment or must have naturalized.

56. It should be noted that naturalization has historically been the result of mixed motives, and decisions to naturalize based primarily on instrumental considerations are likely to yield attachment and loyalty in the long run.

57. It is important to point out that programs that are public and noncontributory in one country may be private and contributory in another country. Health insurance, for example, can fulfill both these criteria. The program description at the end of each table in appendix I indicates whether or not a program is contributory.

58. This evidence is contested. For example, data suggest that noncitizens in Germany are net contributors to the social security system because they tend to be younger than the native population.

59. Alternatively, many politicians in the EU oppose liberalizing the acquisition of citizenship for the very reason that they view citizenship to be the culmination of the integration process rather than a vehicle toward it.

60. Will Kymlicka (1995: 177) offers a telling example of the kind of challenge that policy makers might address to expand minorities' public sector employment. He cites the case of "Sikhs who wanted to join the Royal Canadian Mounted Police, but because of their religious requirements to wear a turban, could not do so unless they were exempted from the usual requirements regarding ceremonial headgear." British schools that require the wearing of uniforms solved one such dilemma by allowing Sikh boys to wear a turban in lieu of the traditional cap providing that the turban was in school colors.

61. See, for example, the Starting Line Group's proposal for expanding the labor market rights for third-country nationals as set out in Article 13 of the Treaty of Amsterdam. The group calls for third-country nationals to enjoy: "Free access to any paid employment of his or her choice . . . *after two years legal employment; (and)* . . .free access to any paid employment or self-employment in any member state *after three years legal employment*" (Chopin and Niessen 1998) [emphasis added].

62. This defense can be used for hiring but not for discharges or layoffs under U.S. law. See Immigration and Nationality Act, § 274B(a)(4).

63. For a detailed and incisive portrait of ethnic minorities and disadvantage that is common to many, see Tariq Modood et al. (1997).

64. In Germany children of permanent residents have the same right as German citizens to scholarships, if they have lawfully worked for five years in Germany or one of their parents has worked in the country during the last six years (Groenendijk, Guild, and Barzilay 2000: 46).

65. With regard to the claimed exceptionalism of U.S. policies, in this regard we would note that in 1998, the federal budget for antidiscrimination enforcement was approximately $600 million dollars. Moreover, this represents the tip of the public sector iceberg as the federal antidiscrimination structure is to a great degree replicated at state and local government levels.

66. Restricting discrimination on the basis of citizenship may also have positive effects on combating racial and ethnic prejudice. In Great Britain and the Netherlands, for example, the inclusion of the prohibition to discriminate on the basis of citizenship, in addition to discrimination on the basis of race or ethnic origin, through the British Race Relations Act of 1976 and the Dutch General Equal Treatment Act of 1994, respectively, has made action against racial discrimination more effective.

# Works Cited

Aleinikoff, T. Alexander, and Douglas Klusmeyer, eds. 2000. *From Migrants to Citizens: Membership in a Changing World.* Washington, D.C.: Carnegie Endowment for International Peace.

———— 2001. *Citizenship Today: Global Perspectives and Practices.* Washington, D.C.: Carnegie Endowment for International Peace.

Australian Bureau of Statistics. 2000. "Australia Now: A Statistical Profile (Population)." See <http://www.abs.gov.au>.

Australian Department of Immigration and Multicultural Affairs. 2000. "Help for Migrants and Refugees Settling in Australia." See <http://www.immi.gov.au>.

Birrell, Bob, and Samantha Evans. 1996. "Recently Arrived Migrants and Social Welfare." *People and Place*, Vol. 4, No. 2 (electronic journal).

Bommes, Michael, Stephen Castles, and Catherine Wihtol de Wenden. 1999. "Post–1947 Migration to Australia and the Socio-Political Incorporation of Migrants." *Imis-Beiträge*, Vol. 13, pp. 13–42.

Borowski, Allan. 2000. Discussion presented at the Transatlantic Workshop on Citizenship and the Rights of Immigrants, European University Institute, Florence, Italy, April 2–4, and subsequent conversations.

Brubaker, William Rogers. 1999. "Membership Without Citizenship: The Economic and Social Rights of Noncitizens." In *Migration and Social Cohesion*, ed. Steven Vertovec, p. 262. Cheltenham, U.K., and Northampton, Mass.: Edward Elgar.

Capps, Randy. 2001. *Hardship among Children of Immigrants: Findings from the 1999 National Survey of America's Families.* Washington, D.C.: Urban Institute Press.

Central Bureau of Statistics, Israel. 2000. "Statistical Abstract of Israel: Population," March 6. See <http://www.cbs.gov.il/shnaton51/shnatone51.htm>.

111

Centrelink. 2000. "Services for People with Special Needs." See <http://
www.centrelink.gov.au/internet/internet.nsf/services/index.htm>.

Chopin, Isabelle, and Jan Niessen, eds. 1998. "Proposals for Legislative Measures to
Combat Racism and to Promote Equal Rights in the European Union." London:
Commission for Racial Equality in collaboration with the Starting Line Group.

Christian, Bryan Paul. 1998. "Immigrant Welfare Entitlements in Cross-National Comparison: The Case of the United States and Germany." Unpublished.

Citizenship and Immigration Canada (CIC). 2000. "Welcome to Canada—What You
Should Know: Basic Services." See <http://cicnet.ci.gc.ca/english/newcomer/wel-
come/wel-04e.html>.

Council of Europe. 1977a. "Protocol Amending the Convention on the Reduction of
Cases of Multiple Nationality and Military Obligations in Cases of Multiple Nationality." November 24, ETS No. 95.

————. 1977b. "Additional Protocol to the Convention on the Reduction of Cases of
Multiple Nationality and Military Obligations in Cases of Multiple Nationality."
November 24, ETS No. 96.

————. 1993. "Second Protocol Amending the Convention on the Reduction of Cases
of Multiple Nationality and Military Obligations in Cases of Multiple Nationality."
February 2, ETS No. 149.

————. 1997. "European Convention on Nationality." November 24, ETS No. 166.

Davy, Ulrike, ed. Forthcoming. *Die Integration von Einwanderern, Band 1: Rechtliche
Regelungen im europäischen Vergleich* [The Integration of Immigrants, Volume
1: Comparing Legal Rules in European States]. Frankfurt, New York: Campus
Verlag.

Dörr, Silvia, and Thomas Faist. 1997. "Institutional Conditions for the Integration of
Immigrants in Welfare States: A Comparison of the Literature on Germany, France,
Great Britain, and the Netherlands." *European Journal of Political Research*, Vol.
31, pp. 401–26.

Faist, Thomas. 2000. "Rights and the Recognition of Immigrants in Welfare States: A
Comparison of Institutional Conditions in Four European Countries." Bremen, Germany: Institute for Intercultural and International Studies, University of Bremen.

Faist, Thomas, and Hartmut Häußermann. 1996. *Immigration, Social Citizenship, and
Housing in Germany*. Abingdon, U.K.: Blackwell Publishers.

Feldblum, Miriam. 2000. "Managing Membership: New Trends in Citizenship and Nationality Policy." In *From Migrants to Citizens: Membership in a Changing World*,
ed. T. Alexander Aleinikoff and Douglas Klusmeyer. Washington, D.C.: Carnegie
Endowment for International Peace.

Fix, Michael, and Jeffrey Passel. 1994. *Immigration and Immigrants: Setting the Record
Straight*. Washington, D.C.: Urban Institute Press.

Fix, Michael, and Wendy Zimmermann. 1999. *All Under One Roof: Mixed Status Families in an Era of Reform*. Washington, D.C.: Urban Institute Press.

Freeman, Gary P., and Nedim Ögelman. 1998. "Homeland Citizenship Policies and the
Status of Third Country Nationals in the European Union." *Journal of Ethnic and
Migration Studies*, Vol. 24, pp. 769, 778–81.

Galloway, Donald. 2000. "The Dilemmas of Canadian Citizenship Law." In *From Migrants to Citizens: Membership in a Changing World*, ed. T. Alexander Aleinikoff

and Douglas Klusmeyer, pp. 82, 86, 99. Washington, D.C.: Carnegie Endowment for International Peace.

Geva-May, Iris. 1996. "Immigration to Israel: Any Lessons for Canada?" Paper presented at Research on Immigration and Integration in the Metropolis (RIIM) conference, Vancouver, Canada.

Gieseck, Arne, Ullrich Heilemann, and Hans Dietrich von Loeffelholz. 1995. "Economic Implications of Migration into the Federal Republic of Germany, 1988–1992." *International Migration Review*, Vol. 29, No. 3, pp. 693–709.

Groenendijk, Kees, Elspeth Guild, and Robin Barzilay. 2001. "The Legal Status of Third-Country Nationals Who Are Long-Term Residents in a Member State of the European Union." Nijmegen, Netherlands: Centre for Migration Law, University of Nijmegen. See <http://www.jur.kun.nl/cmr>.

Hammar, Tomas. 1989. "State, Nation, and Dual Citizenship." In *Immigration and the Politics of Citizenship in Europe and North America*, ed. William Rogers Brubaker, p. 84. New York: University Press of America.

Healy, Ernst. 1996. "Welfare Benefits and Residential Concentrations Amongst Recently Arrived Migrant Communities." *People and Place*, Vol. 4, No. 2 (electronic journal).

Immigration and Naturalization Service (INS). 1999. *1997 Statistical Yearbook of the Immigration and Naturalization Service*, p. 32, table 4. Washington, D.C.: INS.

International Court of Justice. 1955. Nottebohm Case (Liechtenstein v. Guatemala), Second Phase, Judgment, ICJ Reports 1955, Rep. 4, Art. 22–23.

International Covenant on Civil and Political Rights (ICCPR). 1966. 999 U.N.T.S. 171, Art. 18–23. Online at <http://www.unhcr.ch/>.

Jones-Correa, Michael. 2002. "Under Two Flags: Dual Nationality in Latin America and Its Consequences for the United States." In *Rights and Duties of Dual Nationals: Evolution and Prospects*, ed. David A. Martin and Kay Hailbronner. New York: Kluwer Law Publishers.

Joppke, Christian. 1994. "The Domestic Legal Sources of Immigrant Rights: The United States, Germany and the European Union." Working Paper No. SPS 99/3, European University Institute, Badia Fiesolana, Italy.

Khoo, Siew-Ean. 1994. "Correlates of Welfare Dependency Among Immigrants in Australia." *International Migration Review*, Vol. 28, No. 1, pp. 68–90.

Koslowski, Rey. 1998. "European Migration Regimes: Emerging, Enlarging and Deteriorating." *Journal of Ethnic and Migration Studies*, Vol. 24, No. 4, pp. 734, 744.

Kymlicka, Will. 1995. *Multicultural Citizenship: A Liberal Theory of Minority Rights*, p. 177. New York: Oxford University Press.

League of Nations. Treaty Series. 1930. Convention on Certain Questions Relating to the Conflict of Nationality Laws. April 12. *Treaties and International Engagements Registered with the Secretariat of the League of Nations*, Vol. 179, No. 4137 (1937–1938), p. 89.

Legomsky, Stephen H. 2002. "Dual Nationality and Military Service: Strategy Number Two." In *Rights and Duties of Dual Nationals: Evolution and Prospects,* ed. David A. Martin and Kay Hailbronner. New York: Kluwer Law Publishers.

Liebich, André. 2000. "Plural Citizenship in Post-Communist States." *International Journal of Refugee Law*, Vol. 12, No. 1, pp. 103–5.

Lustick, Ian S. 1999. "Israel as a Non-Arab State: The Political Implications of Mass Immigration of Non-Jews." *Middle East Journal*, Vol. 53, No. 3, pp. 417–33.

Markowitz, Fran. 1996. "Living in Limbo: Bosnian Muslim Refugees in Israel." *Human Organization*, Vol. 55, No. 2, pp. 127–32.

Marshall, Thomas Humphrey. 1950. *Citizenship and Social Class and Other Essays*, p. 8. Cambridge, U.K.: Cambridge University Press.

Modood, Tariq, et al. 1997. *Ethnic Minorities in Britain, Diversity and Disadvantage*. London: Policy Studies Institute.

Morris, Lydia. 1998. "Governing at a Distance: The Elaboration of Controls in British Immigration." *International Migration Review*, Vol. 32, No. 4, pp. 949–73.

Murphy, Jill, and Lynn Williams. 1996. "Social Security Recipiency Among Recently Arrived Immigrants." *People and Place*, Vol. 4, No. 2 (electronic journal).

Näir, Sami. 1996. "France: A Crisis of Integration." *Dissent*, Vol. 43 (Summer), pp. 75–8.

National Immigration Law Center (NILC). 1998. "Federal Laws and Implementation." In *Immigrants and Welfare Resource Manual: 1998 Edition*. Washington, D.C.: NILC.

———. 2000. "Overview of Immigrant Eligibility for Federal Programs." In *Building Immigrant Opportunities 2000—Public Benefit and Employment Strategies in the New Economy* (National Conference Binder). Washington, D.C.: NILC.

Passel, Jeffrey, and Jennifer Van Hook. 2000. *The Adult Children of Immigrants: Integration of the Second Generation*. Washington, D.C.: Urban Institute Press.

Pendakur, Ravi. 2000. "Canada." Prepared for the Transatlantic Workshop on Citizenship and the Rights of Immigrants. Ottawa: Canadian Heritage.

Rosenhek, Zeev. 1998. "Migration Regimes, Intra-State Conflicts and the Politics of Exclusion and Inclusion: Migrant Workers in the Israeli Welfare State." Paper presented at the Third International Metropolis conference.

Scott, James Brown. 2000. *Proceedings of the Hague Peace Conferences: Translations of the Official Texts*, pp. 368, 389. New York: William S. Hein and Company.

Shachar, Ayelet. 2000. "Citizenship and Membership in the Israeli Polity." In *From Migrants to Citizens: Membership in a Changing World*, ed. T. Alexander Aleinikoff and Douglas Klusmeyer, pp. 386–433. Washington, D.C.: Carnegie Endowment for International Peace.

Smith, David M., and Maurice Blanc. 1996. "Citizenship, Nationality, and Ethnic Minorities in Three European Nations." *International Journal of Urban and Regional Research*, Vol. 20, pp. 66–82.

SOPEMI. 1999. *Trends in International Migration, 1999*. Paris: Organization for Economic Cooperation and Development.

Soysal, Yasemin. 1994. *Limits of Citizenship: Migrants and Postnational Membership in Europe*. Chicago, Ill.: University of Chicago Press.

United Kingdom. 2000a. R v. London Borough of Wandsworth, ex parte O, Court of Appeal (Civil Division), LGR 591.

———. 2000b. R v. Leicester City Council, ex parte Bikha, Court of Appeal (Civil Division), LGR 591.

United Nations. 1948. Universal Declaration of Human Rights. New York: United Nations, Art. 18–20. <http://www.un.org/Overview/rights.html>.

United Nations. Secretariat. 2000. Department of Economic and Social Affairs, Population Division. *Replacement Migration: Is It a Solution to Declining and Ageing Populations?* See <http://www.un.org/esa/population/unpop.htm>.

United Nations. Treaty Series (UNTS). 1957. Convention on the Nationality of Married Women, February 20. *Treaties and International Agreements Registered or Filed and Recorded with the Secretariat of the United Nations*, Vol. 309, No. 4468, Art. 1, p. 65.

———. Treaty Series (UNTS). 1961. Agreement on Dual Nationality Spain-Bolivia. La Paz, October 12. *Treaties and International Engagements Registered with the Secretariat of the League of Nations*, Vol. 954, No. 13669, p. 379.

———. Treaty Series (UNTS). 1963. Convention on the Reduction of Cases of Multiple Nationality and Military Obligations in Cases of Multiple Nationality. May 6. *Treaties and International Agreements Registered or Filed and Recorded with the Secretariat of the United Nations*, Vol. 634, No. 9065, p. 221.

———. Treaty Series (UNTS). 1979. Convention on the Elimination of All Forms of Discrimination against Women. December 18. *Treaties and International Agreements Registered or Filed and Recorded with the Secretariat of the United Nations*, Vol. 1249, No. 20378, Art. 9, p. 13.

———. Treaty Series (UNTS). 1979. "Agreement on Nationality Spain-Colombia." Madrid, June 27. *Treaties and International Engagements Registered with the Secretariat of the League of Nations*, Vol. 1206, No. 19299, p. 47.

United States. 1972. Rogers v. Bellei, 401 U.S. 815, 832.

———. 1973. Sugarman v. Dougall, 413 U.S. 634.

———. 1979. Ambach v. Norwick, 441 U.S. 68.

———. 1978. Foley v. Connelie, 435 U.S. 291.

———. 1982. Cabell v. Chavez-Salido, 454 U.S. 432.

Urban Institute. 1998. *Tabulations of March 1998 Current Population Survey*. Washington, D.C.: Urban Institute Press.

Vermeulen, Hans, ed. 1997. *Immigration Policy for a Multicultural Society: A Comparative Study of Integration, Language and Religious Policy in Five Western European Countries*. Brussels: Migration Policy Group.

Waldrauch, Harald. 2000. "The Rights of Immigrants: Employment and Social Benefits: Tables Prepared for the Transatlantic Workshop on Citizenship and the Rights of Immigrants." Vienna: European Centre for Social Welfare Policy and Research.

———, ed. Forthcoming. *Die Integration von Einwanderern, Band 2: Ein Index legaler Diskriminierung* [The Integration of Immigrants, Volume 2: An Index of Legal Discrimination]. Frankfurt, New York: Campus Verlag.

Weil, Patrick. 2001. "Access to Citizenship: A Comparison of Twenty-Five Nationality Laws." In *Citizenship Today: Global Perspectives and Practices*, ed. T. Alexander Aleinikoff and Douglas Klusmeyer, pp. 22–3. Washington, D.C.: Carnegie Endowment for International Peace.

Wenzel, Uwe, and Mathias Bös. 1997. "Immigration and the Modern Welfare State: The Case of the USA and Germany." *New Community*, Vol. 23, No. 4, pp. 537–48.

Wrench, John. 1996. *Preventing Racism in the Workplace: A Report on 16 European Countries*. Dublin: European Foundation for the Improvement of Living and Working Conditions.

Wrench, John, Andrea Rea, and Nouria Ouali. 1999. *Migrants, Ethnic Minorities and the Labour Market: Integration and Exclusion in Europe*. Warwick, U.K.: Centre for Research in Ethnic Relations. See <http://www.warwick.ac.uk/fac/soc/CRER_RC/publications>.

Zappalà, Gianni, and Stephen Castles. 2000. "Citizenship and Immigration in Australia." In *From Migrants to Citizens: Membership in a Changing World*, ed. T. Alexander Aleinikoff and Douglas Klusmeyer, pp. 46–7. Washington, D.C.: Carnegie Endowment for International Peace.

Zimmermann, Wendy, and Karen C. Tumlin. 1999. *Patchwork Policies: State Assistance for Immigrants Under Welfare Reform*. Washington, D.C.: Urban Institute Press.

Zlotnik, Hania. 1998. "International Migration 1965–96: An Overview." *Population and Development Review*, Vol. 24, No. 3, pp. 429–68.

# Index

The Migration Policy Institute (MPI) is an independent, nonpartisan, nonprofit think tank dedicated to the study of the movement of people worldwide. The Institute provides knowledge-based policy analysis, development, and evaluation of migration and refugee issues at the local, national, and international levels. It aims to meet the rising demand for pragmatic responses to the challenges and opportunities that large-scale migration, whether voluntary or forced, presents to communities and institutions in an ever more integrated world. MPI grew out of the International Migration Policy Program of the Carnegie Endowment for International Peace, founded in 1989, which provided analytical and intellectual guidance to a number of the most important migration policy debates of the 1990s.

MPI's work is organized around four thematic pillars. Under the first, *Migration Management*, MPI focuses on how different states manage the flows of people across their borders and how their social institutions adapt to these flows. In the second pillar, *Refugee Protection and International Human Rights*, MPI uses a combination of legal and social science research to track new developments in thinking, law, and practice in the realm of refugee protection, and proposes ways to reconcile the protection needs of refugees and the policy priorities of sovereign states. The *North American Borders and Migration Agenda*, the third pillar, enables MPI to use the results of its extensive research to provide an intellectual framework for discussing concrete steps toward cooperative management of common borders and movements of people in North America. Finally, through its *Immigrant Settlement and Integration* pillar, MPI works with researchers, advocates, and officials of national, state, and local governments to understand better how newcomers and receiving communities interact, and to develop an analytical framework and a plan of action for improving this interaction for the benefit of all.

Migration Policy Institute
1400 16th St., NW, Suite 300
Washington, D.C. 20036-2257
202-266-1940
www.migrationpolicy.org